COACHING FROM MY WHEELCHAIR

Tips, Tidbits, Tools, and Strategies for Improving Your Personal and Professional Self-Development

Dr. Les Wright, Jr., BCC

ISBN: 978-1-962624-07-7

Dedication

This work is dedicated to all who buy this book; thank you for giving my words a chance. May you find something that speaks to you personally within these chapters.

Acknowledgments

I want to thank my family for significantly impacting my life and instilling in me the drive to be the best version of myself. I am most grateful to Steve for giving me the support, encouragement, space, and time to put my thoughts to paper and succeed in writing this book. I want to thank my peer coaches, mentors, faculty members, and coaching trainers from my coaching certification programs. They have all contributed in some way to my personal and professional growth, which have made this book possible. I would also like to thank my past and present coaching clients and mentees, from whom I have learned much from their shared experiences. I hope they have learned from me as much as I have learned from them in their pursuit of their self-development.

Table of Contents

About the Author

Dr. Les Wright is a veteran educator and leader with over 20 years of experience in educational leadership, training, and program management in higher education administration and the federal government.

In 2020, Dr. Wright retired early from the federal government (i.e., NASA) due to the progression of his muscular dystrophy (MD), a disease that causes weakness and loss of muscle mass.

Unfortunately, there is no cure, but medications and therapy can help manage symptoms and slow the course of the disease (Dimachkie & Barohn, 2014).

Dr. Wright currently uses a wheelchair, having lost the ability to walk independently. Despite his challenges and limitations, Dr. Wright remains active and engaged as the CEO and owner of the Wright Coaching and Consulting Services LLC, a veteran-owned small business that helps individuals, professionals, and leaders develop their skills, improve their strengths, and design a plan to achieve their goals through personal, professional, and executive leadership coaching.

Dr. Wright's coaching and consulting services focus on enhancing clients' self-discovery and individual awareness, setting goals, achieving a work–life balance, and managing change.

Dr. Wright is a board-certified coach credentialed by the Center for Credentialing & Education and holds a graduate certificate in evidence-based executive coaching. He is a certified DISC behavior analyst with coaching certifications and credentials through Taking Flight Learning.

In addition to his coaching and consulting work, Dr. Wright is an active volunteer for a veteran's nonprofit organization, where he serves as an advisor, mentor, and career coach to veterans around the country who seek advice and tools for long-term career development through mentoring, counseling, and networking.

Additionally, he serves on the board of directors of the Our Cause Education and Scholarship Foundation.

Dr. Wright is a member of Phi Beta Sigma Fraternity, Inc., the Society for Industrial and Organizational Psychology, the American Evaluation Association, and the American Psychological Association. He also served 4 years in the U.S. Army. He has a doctorate in higher education and adult learning from Walden University, a master's degree in adult education and instructional technology from Troy University, and a bachelor's degree from Louisiana Tech University.

Defying the challenges posed by MD, Dr. Wright remains committed to helping others achieve their full potential through his coaching, consulting work, and volunteer activities.

Chapter One

Introduction

Welcome to Coaching From My Wheelchair: Tips, Tidbits, Tools, and Strategies for Improving Your Personal and Professional Self-Development!

Every day is an opportunity for a new beginning—a chance to seek change and grow into the person you've always wanted to be. There is no better time than the present to commit to caring for yourself in the best way you possibly can. This book is here to help you tap into your inner strength, overcome obstacles, and unleash the best version of yourself. Whether you want to improve your career, relationships, or personal growth, you've come to the right place!

This book is not just about knowledge but transformation, empowerment, and fulfilling your dreams. I am here to inspire, motivate, and encourage you to make those things happen. I am here to help turn your "I wish" into "I will" and your "someday" into "today." Do you need help in your personal or professional development? Are you going through a difficult or challenging time and looking for a source of inspiration or guidance?

You're not alone! This book is designed specifically for you—anyone looking to make positive changes in their lives.

As a coach, I aim to help you develop self-awareness by asking probing questions about your thoughts, behaviors, and beliefs. Pursuing answers to these questions can help you achieve the results you desire.

This book outlines strategies, tips, and tools, as well as a few tidbits to help you stay focused—which are especially helpful when you feel like you've hit a brick wall—and it provides ways to overcome negative thoughts and feelings that may be holding you back. By viewing your life through someone else's lens, you will gain a fresh perspective and find new ways to tackle challenges.

I hope that this book will empower you to get the most out of your job, relationship, family life, and community. Together, we'll work toward your goals using a positive psychology and humanistic approach—with the *GROW* model, which stands for "goals," "reality," "options," and "will." I can help you raise awareness and responsibility by asking you the following questions: What do you want? Where are you now? What could you do? What will you do? Additionally, I will provide you with the tools and structure to achieve your goals and stay on the right track (Whitmore, 2017).

Each chapter of this book covers coaching trends and common topics from my coaching experiences, personal encounters, evidence- based research, and related articles. In addition, you will receive practical tips, tidbits, tools, and strategies to help you stay focused, build confidence, and discover the power of positive thinking to set and achieve your goals—which is especially helpful for improving your personal and professional self-development. I aim to inspire you to become a warrior of self-discovery and achieve your desired goal. Let's work together so that you become a better version of yourself, and let this book be your guide on the path toward self-improvement.

I have dedicated most of my professional life to helping people unlock their full potential and achieve their dreams. My passion for empowering individuals shines through every word I write, and my unique approach to personal development has inspired countless people to live life on their own terms, chase their dreams with relentless passion, and make a positive impact within their work, personal life, and community.

I have an unwavering commitment to helping others seek self-improvement. Throughout my career, I have helped people overcome their fears, break free from limiting beliefs, and unleash their inner potential.

I will let you in on my secret sauce (not the one I use for my gumbo but for my approach to self-development): it is a blend of evidence-based coaching, mentoring, researching, and implementing best practices that are rooted in the belief that every person has the potential to achieve greatness.

I firmly believe in the power of positive thinking and the impression that our thoughts and beliefs have on our lives. Therefore, I have developed a series of distinct tools and techniques that help individuals tap into their inner abilities, and my methods are designed to help people achieve their full potential and live their best lives.

Picture this: an accomplished educator, trainer, mentor, and coach who enjoys helping people overcome their struggles and achieve their goals suddenly realizes he has a story of his own to tell— a story that's not only about him but about all of us and the power to overcome adversity and reach new heights.

I've finally put pen to paper and written the book that's been burning in my heart for so long. So, what *finally* lit the spark? As I watched the world grapple with the COVID-19 pandemic, I couldn't help but feel that coaching was going to become even more important, as it brought with it a unique set of challenges to help people set goals, make better decisions, and take action in their personal life and career.

That's why I decided to go back to school and become certified in evidence-based coaching—and I'm not alone! Many coaches like me are entering the field and bringing academic rigor and theory to their practice. This was a great opportunity to showcase the power of coaching with clients by sharing relevant studies and testimonials about how coaching can help many people navigate challenging times. Thanks to the rise of web conferencing and online meeting systems such as Zoom and WebEx, I can work from home or anywhere in the world—which is especially important for me as a disabled veteran who uses a wheelchair.

Additionally, with so many people now accustomed to remote work relationships and virtual meetings, it just makes sense for coaches to leverage technology in the same way. Research has shown that technology has the potential to impact coaching by transforming the way coaches engage our clients, requiring increased flexibility (Pascal et al., 2015).

It is important to stay ahead of the latest technologies, especially in a highly communicative industry such as coaching. The pandemic reminded us how technology can keep us connected, even when we are forced to be socially distant.

I've gathered insights and ideas about personal and professional leadership through running my coaching practice, writing self-development articles for my hometown's local newspaper in Colfax, Louisiana, training to attain credentials and certification, and learning from my colleagues.

Now, I've distilled them all into this book. I hope that by reading it, you'll feel inspired to become an expert self-developer in your own right and unlock your full potential!

As a lifelong learner, I have witnessed the power of positive thinking. I have also seen how often people struggle with self-doubt, fear, and negativity, which prevents them from realizing their strengths.

This is where the pun comes in: I wanted to point a light in the "Wright" direction (Ha!) for those seeking motivation and inspiration. I wanted to write a book that would not only provide practical tips and strategies for success but also bring a smile to the reader's face.

The key inspiration behind this book was my own journey to success. I have faced many challenges in my life, but I've never let them stop me from pursuing my dreams. Instead, I've used these meaningful experiences as opportunities to grow and become a better person. I want to share this message with others so that it may resonate with them and help them achieve their own personal success. The countless people I have met who were in their quest for answers—about life, the world, and why and how everything unfolds—have collectively been another major inspiration. These individuals were looking for a way to achieve their goals, improve their lives, and make sense of their life experiences, but they didn't know where to start. They were seeking guidance and someone to show them the way. If this sounds familiar, then this book is for you!

This book will help you see things in a new light. It's a journey of self-discovery and growth, and I sincerely hope that it will nudge you in the "Wright" direction to make positive changes in your life.

You'll be given practical tips and strategies for overcoming self-doubt and building confidence, as well as methods for setting and achieving your goals. You'll also discover the power of positive thinking, the importance of self-care, and ways to build strong, healthy relationships.

Let me tell you something. You don't always have to reinvent the wheel to achieve success. That's why I wrote this book—to share with you some practical techniques that others have already presented, with my own personal spin.

With the tips and strategies outlined in these pages, you can add energy to your life to develop the drive you need to chase your dreams and make them a reality.

Now, here's the thing: success means something different to everyone. That's why it's so important to figure out what it means to *you*. That's exactly what this book will help you do.

This book will provide you with constructive and actionable information on the tools you need to do the following:

Inject some positivity into your life. Crush obstacles with a can-do attitude.

Manage change like a pro.

Seek out opportunities to learn and grow. Step outside your comfort zone and take risks.

Boost your self-awareness and take control of your life.

Create a routine that works for you in just three simple steps.

Understand the people around you so that you can communicate with them more effectively.

Whether you're looking for a motivational guide to help you reach your goals or are just plain curious about personal development, this book has something for you.

Let it be the ultimate guide to unlocking your true potential. Whether you're a seasoned personal development enthusiast or just starting your journey, these insights are sure to help you live your life to the fullest.

So, buckle up and get ready for an exciting journey ahead!

Chapter Two

The Power of Positivity

"The problem is not the problem; the problem is your attitude about the problem."

Captain Jack Sparrow

You've probably heard the saying, "positive vibes only." Although it may sound cliché, there's a lot of value in it. When we focus on the positive aspects of our lives, we're better equipped to handle challenges, build resilience, and create a sense of happiness and fulfillment.

In this chapter, we will explore the benefits of positive thinking, learn how a positive mindset can transform your life, and dissect the practical tips for cultivating a positive mindset.

I was at a training workshop a few years ago, when during one of the breaks, I began a conversation with a man—let's call him Neil. As the conversation went on, I began to feel drained. Neil was finding everything wrong with the training workshop, whining about how mad he was because his boss made him attend it even though he supposedly knew everything already. Neil did not see the good in anything related to the workshop.

I wanted to say to him, "Dude, shut up! You're killing me." You might be thinking, "Yes, this has been me at times," and as you're reading this, someone you have been in a similar situation with might immediately come to mind.

People like Neil often spend too much time focusing on things in their lives that don't make them happy, whether it be their career, family, relationship, lifestyle, or health. Rather than focusing on the good in a situation and identifying changes that could be made to improve it further, they would rather complain about how awful everything is. As a result, these people may find themselves in a negative feedback loop.

What Exactly Is Negativity, and What Makes It So Dangerous?

Negativity is a state of mind wherein we focus on worst-case scenarios instead of the positive outcomes that are possible. It's a way of thinking that is filled with doubt, fear, and pessimism. When we adopt a negative mindset, we close ourselves off from the possibilities that exist in the world around us.

Think of negativity as a toxic virus that infects the mind, spreading its damaging effects to every aspect of our lives. It's a pervasive and destructive force that can ruin even the most promising opportunities and relationships.

The influence of negative thoughts is far-reaching. There's no part of your life that escapes it. We all know at least one person who acts like a negative Nancy—or negative Neil.

Although this type of person isn't fun to be around, you might not realize that they can negatively affect your own happiness, success, and health, limiting your ability to enjoy life.

What Are Some Dangers of Negativity?

Negativity can cause us to miss out on opportunities, productivity, and success. When we focus on the negative, we become blind to the potential for success and growth. We become so caught up in our fears and doubts we fail to take action or seize the moment when opportunities arise.

Have you ever noticed how much time you spend thinking about negative or painful situations, ruminating on, or replaying what's not working?

Negative thinking is exhausting; it saps your energy and your resources. Negative emotions can also lead to decreased motivation and energy, making it difficult to focus and complete tasks (Baumeister et al., 2007). In addition, negative emotions can affect our decision-making abilities, leading to poor choices and outcomes (Lerner & Keltner, 2001).

It's Not Just You

Strangely, the more negative an experience, the more often we may return to it. Like vultures to a carcass, we're often drawn to what hurts.

I spent years letting my negativity about having MD run my life, experiencing each of its dangers at one time or another, including regret. Although I am a long way from the end of my days (I hope), I regret missed opportunities.

Negativity can also be toxic to your relationships and lead to a lack of connection with others. When we adopt a negative mindset, we tend to see the worst in others. We become overly critical, judgmental, and defensive. We push people away, sabotaging our chances for meaningful relationships. Negative emotions, such as anger and resentment, can erode relationships (Fincham & Beach, 2010).

This bad stuff will stick in our minds, hearts, and bodies much more easily than the good stuff! We tend to "get off on" and react more strongly to negative interactions than positive ones.

This can dramatically skew your perception of your spouse, significant other, coworker, or friend and potentially blind you to the good things they have to offer as well as the good times you've shared. This is why one insult may affect you more than five compliments and why you may lie awake at night angry at the world, dwelling on all the unpleasant events of your life instead of remembering the good ones. Negativity can also take the joy out of life by profoundly impacting our mental and physical health. Stress and anxiety, often caused by negative emotions, can increase the risk of heart disease, stroke, and other health problems (Kivimäki et al., 2012). They can also weaken the immune system, making us more susceptible to illness and infection (Glaser & Kiecolt-Glaser, 2005).

According to *Psychology Today*, negative thoughts significantly impact brain function. Not only does negative thinking make it more difficult to think logically, but the fear of failure often associated with negativity slows down activity in the cerebellum. This results in a reduced ability to develop creative solutions to the problems you face. The fear of failure that negative thinkers often carry also affects the brain's left temporal lobe; not only do fears drag your mood down, but you may also suffer from bad memory or poor impulse control.

When you make a habit of negative thinking, you are essentially rewiring your brain. As you focus on these fears and worries, the brain begins to change, strengthening the synapses and neurons most closely associated with negative thoughts. These changes are what make it so difficult to overcome a negative attitude. You aren't simply working to correct negative thoughts—you are working against thoughts and beliefs that have become part of the structure of your brain.

To add fuel to the fire, negativity lowers self-esteem. When you think you're overweight, unattractive, or incapable, it's damaging to your self-esteem. Not everyone who engages in negative thinking has a mental or physical health problem—just as not everyone with a mental or physical health issue suffers from constant negative thoughts. However, negative thinking can be detrimental to your health and quality of life, particularly when you let it take you over.

I Won't Sugarcoat It

Negativity is a part of life. It's difficult to combat and can become a habit. However, adopting a positive outlook has immediate advantages that will benefit both you and those around you.

Consider this: rather than feeling negative every day, imagine resetting your beliefs and enhancing your positive thoughts to overcome challenges and achieve your life goals. The simple fact is you can. This is a choice you can make, and the outcome you reach will be a direct reflection of that choice.

I am a staunch believer in the power of positivity and positive psychology, and I have seen miraculous changes in people's lives when they switch to a more positive mindset. My goal is to help you face the dangers of negativity and avoid its long-term ramifications, for which I've developed several tools and strategies.

How Can We Overcome Negativity and Its Dangers?

The answer lies in the power of positivity.

We experience a variety of emotions that directly impact our choices and self-perception. A bad experience can result in negative thinking, which can be detrimental to a person's self-confidence and outlook on life.

This is why positive thinking is so powerful. Establishing a positive attitude can be challenging at times, but through practice and encouragement, it becomes a skill that can shape and transform your life.

As a coach, I take a positive psychology approach with my clients to identify solutions to help them explore their values, strengths, weaknesses, resilience, and resourcefulness to increase well-being, enhance and apply strengths, improve performance, and achieve goals. Exploring negative experiences is a core component of positive psychology. Understanding negative thoughts and behaviors versus positive ones and those that are needed to achieve objectives are at the heart of my approach.

Now you must be wondering: what exactly is positivity?

Positivity is a state of mind that involves seeing the good in people, situations, and life.

It's about focusing on what's going well rather than dwelling on what's going wrong. Positivity doesn't mean ignoring problems or pretending everything is perfect. Instead, it's about facing challenges with a positive attitude and finding ways to overcome them.

Positivity can help you develop an optimistic outlook on life, increase resilience, and improve your overall well-being. Building positivity is not a one-time task; it is an ongoing process that requires effort and commitment.

Positivity can help us see the world in a different light. Instead of focusing on the negative, we begin to look for the positive.

A positive mindset is one of the most essential strategies for moving past obstacles in your life. It can change the way you think, feel, and act. It increases your confidence in overcoming enormous challenges and keeps your mind open to new possibilities and ways of dealing with problems. As a result, we start to see the opportunities around us, and we become willing to take risks and pursue our dreams.

Positivity can also help us build better relationships. When we adopt a positive mindset, we become open and accepting of others. We become compassionate and empathetic, and we connect meaningfully with others.

Although we can't control potential setbacks, we can control how we react to them and whether we accept defeat. Be kind to yourself in challenging moments. Take control of the situation and keep moving forward.

There are seven practical strategies you can use to cultivate positivity in your life. If you want to be a more effective positive thinker, you'll need concrete tips and techniques to help you through the process.

1. *Start Your Day With a Positive Attitude*

How you start the morning sets the tone for the rest of the day. Have you ever woken up late, panicked, dropped your phone, chosen the wrong outfit, shouted at your hair, argued with your significant other over nothing, and then, to top it all off, the car wouldn't start? And by the end of the day, you found yourself feeling like nothing good happened all day?

This is likely because you started the day with a pessimistic attitude, and it carried over into every other situation you found yourself in.

Instead of letting negative events dominate you, start your day with positive affirmations, even amid early morning challenges. When a negative event happens, stop for a minute, and take a deep breath to recenter yourself.

Talk to yourself in the mirror, even if you feel silly, and say things like, "Today will be a good day" or "Today is starting out a little rough, but I've got this."

It might feel strange at first, but talking to yourself can influence your thoughts, feelings, and behavior—especially if you're speaking to yourself in the second or third person. Try it—you'll be amazed at how much your day improves!

2. *Turn Failures Into Lessons, and Focus on Your Strengths*

You aren't perfect. But you're perfect for you. You will make mistakes and experience failure. Yet, instead of focusing on how you failed, think about what you might change the next time—turn your failure into a lesson. For example, you might say to yourself, "I bombed the workshop presentation. My speech was all over the place, and I felt like crap afterward."

Sometimes we continually replay or dissect an upsetting event in the past or even think about the possibility of negative situations in the future. Every once in a while, you might still get knots in your stomach over a not-so-stellar presentation.

Rather than fixating on the problem itself, focus on your strengths, the positive qualities you possess, and those that can help you prevent the negative experience from repeating itself. Research has shown that focusing on strengths can increase positive emotions, self-esteem, and overall well-being (Wood et al., 2011).

Take time to reflect on your strengths and consider how you can use them to achieve your goals.

3. *Focus on the Now by Practicing Mindfulness*

I'm talking about the present—not today or this hour—but this exact moment. You may be getting chewed out by your boss or fighting with your spouse, or perhaps your best friend is getting on your nerves. In moments like these, think about what is happening in this exact moment that is so bad.

Forget the comment someone made 5 minutes ago. Forget what they might say 5 minutes from now. Focus on this one individual moment. In most situations, you'll find that it's not as bad as you imagine. Most sources of negativity stem from a memory of a recent event or the exaggerated imagination of a future event.

We can cultivate positivity by practicing mindfulness. Mindfulness is the practice of being present in the moment, and it can help us become aware of our thoughts and emotions.

Mindfulness involves focusing on the present without becoming overly reactive to or being overwhelmed by your circumstances. By noticing our negative thoughts and choosing to replace them with positive ones, we can train our minds to think positively. Therefore, instead of dwelling on the past or worrying about the future, it will allow you to focus on the present moment. It will help you appreciate the here and now and reduce anxiety.

Mindfulness is an essential component of cultivating a happy, meaningful life. The more aware you are of your feelings, the more likely you will find and maintain your center.

4. *Laugh at Yourself and Find the Humor in Bad Situations*

Allow yourself to experience humor even in the darkest or most trying situations. I remember when I first started to sense that something was wrong with my muscles. I was in the military at the time. It was a comfortable morning, and our battalion was preparing for a 2-mile run. I was not the best of runners but not the worst either. When we were a little more than halfway through, I began to feel cramps in my legs, and I suddenly collapsed and began to spasm for a few minutes. Eventually, I got up and walked with assistance. I was taken to a small clinic on base, and after a few medical tests, the doctors discovered an issue with my muscles.

At the time, negative thoughts swirled through my mind. I recall wondering whether it was related to the condition that plagued my dad and some of his siblings.

It wasn't until after specialists ran tests that I found out I had a form of MD. Of course, I researched it and talked to my parents to decipher what it was and what effect it would have on my body. The verdict was not good: MD is a terminal disease.

There's no cure for it, and the only thing doctors can do is make your life comfortable and manageable until the inevitable happens. With this newfound information, I had my pity party and sat with my negative thoughts. I sat in my barracks room, but after a while, I just chuckled. I thought, "Look on the bright side. You get to do modified physical training, and you don't have to do a company or battalion run again."

You might think of this as disrespectful to others suffering from MD, but I mean no disrespect. That day was one of the saddest and heaviest of my life. The point of laughing and finding humor in it wasn't to make the pain go away forever or avoid what was necessary to confront—it was to use humor as a coping mechanism. It is a tool for creating positive energy.

Studies have shown that laughter and humor have multiple benefits, including strengthening the immune system, reducing pain and stress, and increasing positive energy. By using humor strategically and finding it in things regularly, you will build a mental muscle that is attuned with some form of levity to present throughout your day (Louie et al., 2016).

Just like anything else you pay attention to, where focus goes, energy flows, so you will begin to see more of what you want to see. If you are going through a difficult experience, humor may accidentally find you. If you embrace it, those negative thoughts in your life may not seem quite as overwhelming.

Even in the darkest, most trying, and most difficult moments, if something is funny, you have to laugh—even at yourself. Seize the opportunity to escape a negative situation, if only briefly, and welcome the release.

5. *Practice Gratitude, and Choose to Be Positive*

One of the most effective ways to build positivity is to concentrate on gratitude. Gratitude is the practice of focusing on the good things in our lives, and it's a powerful way to shift from a negative mindset to a positive one.

It's natural to feel upset, fearful, mad, confused, or frustrated when faced with a challenge. Our bodies are hardwired to feel these emotions. It's understandable that gratitude may not be at the forefront of your mind, but it can be helpful even in the worst situations.

So, although negative emotions come naturally and frequently, they don't have to stay. What you choose to focus on will endure. I have found this to be true with gratitude. The more you practice positive thinking, the more it is reinforced. As you focus on gratitude, you may begin to find yourself operating in that mindset naturally in the future.

Take time each day to reflect on the good things in your life. Practicing gratitude can be as simple as writing a thank you card, meditating through prayer and reading the Bible, or documenting your thoughts in a journal.

As a person of faith, giving thanks and praise gives me hope. Realizing how significant God's influence is helps me understand how insignificant my complaints and negative thoughts are by comparison.

When you focus on the blessings and good things in your life, you will appreciate them more and develop a more positive outlook.

6. *Spend Time With Those Who Uplift and Inspire You*

Make an effort to build and maintain positive relationships with family, friends, and colleagues. Avoid negative or toxic relationships that drain your energy and make you unhappy. Instead, spend time with those who uplift and inspire you.

This practice can help you maintain a positive outlook and overcome challenges. Positive people tend to be optimistic, enthusiastic, and supportive. Through one of my social media group blogs and chat sites, I have learned that many people in the disability community are mentally strong and confident and have high self- esteem.

Although some people look upon those with disabilities with pity, we refuse to focus wholly on this one aspect of our lives, choosing instead to be grateful for the parts of our body that function well. Within our community, we absorb positive energy from one another and see the world in a positive light.

Take time to reflect on those with whom you surround yourself.

Do they give you positive or negative energy?

You are worthy of surrounding yourself with positive people who bring out the best in you. When you do this, you will adopt empowering values, best practices, and beliefs and see the many positive things happening for you.

7. *Engage in Activities That Bring You Joy*

Whether it is spending time in nature, pursuing a hobby, spending time with loved ones, or engaging in activities you enjoy, these pastimes can increase positive emotions and overall well-being (Fredrickson, 2001).

I recently helped one of my clients, who is a parent, with work– life balance concerns. I asked her how things were going, how her home life was, and whether there were problems or worries I should know about. She expressed how she was dealing with her daughter who is exhibiting a lot of negativity. She told me that it was never easy to hear her child express negative thoughts or see her wallow in feelings such as self-doubt, sadness, or anger.

"This negativity," I told her, "is usually driven by fear, doubt, or shame, all of which produce stress chemicals in the brain. A negative attitude can ultimately shape how a child sees herself and the world around her." The parent and I then worked on strategies and activities to create a plan that would render positive results for both of them.

There is plenty we can do to help our children the same way we help ourselves. Adults can develop a positive attitude about themselves and their world. I suggested that she could accomplish this by encouraging her daughter to engage in exercises aimed at helping her rewire her brain. One of the most powerful ways to encourage a positive attitude is to model this behavior. When you accept and process your emotions in a healthy way, you show others how to do the same. Watch a funny movie, share a funny joke or good news, or engage in physical affection. Anything that sparks feelings of joy, contentment, and love contributes to positive thinking, especially when these emotions are shared.

Make time for activities that bring you contentment and prioritize them in your life. Regular exercise, healthy eating, and plentiful sleep are essential for maintaining positive emotions and overall well-being (Huang et al., 2016).

Do something nice for yourself: take a bubble bath, sleep in, or treat yourself to your favorite meal. Being nice to yourself will help you increase your self-love, and you will feel relaxed and happier. If weighing yourself is a make-or-break moment in your day, put the scale away in the closet because your health and happiness are not defined by it. Focus on taking care of yourself—mind, body, and soul.

I bet you will feel more positive and energized.

Final Thoughts

The power of positivity lies in its ability to shape our perception of the world. When we have a positive outlook, we are more likely to see opportunities instead of obstacles and approach challenges with a growth mindset. This can lead to increased creativity, productivity, and overall success (Dweck, 2006).

Remember that positivity is not just a mindset but a lifestyle; it takes time and effort to develop. However, the benefits of positivity are worth it—increased happiness, better relationships, and improved overall well-being.

You can cultivate positivity and improve your overall well- being by focusing on gratitude, strengths, positive relationships, enjoyable activities, and self-care. Remember that building positivity is a journey, and making mistakes is okay. The important thing is to keep moving forward and stay committed to your goals.

You now know the dangers of negativity and the power of positivity. You know how to develop positivity in your life, including practicing gratitude, mindfulness, and self-compassion. You've also learned to handle negativity and setbacks by reframing your thoughts and using positive self-talk.

But we're not going to stop here!

Keep practicing and incorporating positivity into your daily routine. Surround yourself with positive people and environments. Continue to educate yourself on positivity and personal development by reading books and articles, attending seminars, or working with a coach.

Remember, you can choose how you view the world and your life by choosing to focus on the negative or positive side of things. Choose positivity, and watch your life transform into a more joyful and fulfilling experience.

If you do one thing today, go out there and spread positivity! You've got this!

Chapter Three

Obstacles Are Inevitable

"Success is to be measured not so much by the position that one has reached in life as by the obstacles which he has overcome."

— *Booker T. Washington*

In this chapter, we will discuss an unpleasant topic but one that is fundamental to your success: obstacles.

You will face obstacles no matter who you are or what you want to accomplish. It's how you handle those obstacles that will determine your level of success.

Obstacles can come in many forms, from a difficult exam to a challenging project at work to personal issues that affect your ability to focus. They can seem insurmountable, so it's easy to feel discouraged when faced with them.

However, the truth is that obstacles are a natural part of the journey to success. No one has ever achieved anything truly worthwhile without facing some obstacles along the way.

Obstacles are not roadblocks; they're simply detours on your path to success. They are opportunities to learn and grow.

Obstacles don't have to hold you back. In fact, they can be the very things that push you forward and make you stronger. When you encounter an obstacle, think of it as a chance to develop grit and resilience, which are two essential qualities for achieving success.

Don't let an obstacle become the focus of your attention. Instead, focus on finding a way around it. Think creatively and be willing to adapt your approach.

Think of an obstacle as a challenge that's been put in your path to test your resolve. How you handle that challenge is up to you— you can let it defeat you, or you can use it as a steppingstone to greatness. It's all a matter of perspective.

Remember, there is always a solution, even if it's not immediately obvious.

Experiencing obstacles in life can bring along a lot of negativities. It feels as if, suddenly, your whole world is crashing down.

So, What Should You Do?

First, let's acknowledge that obstacles are a part of life. No matter who you are, where you come from, or what you're trying to do, you will inevitably run into setbacks. It's just the way the universe works. When we're faced with obstacles, it's natural to feel discouraged, frustrated, or even defeated. It's only human.

Prepare yourself mentally for the fact that there will be bumps in the road and be ready to face them head-on.

When we allow negative emotions to take over, obstacles can start to feel bigger and more insurmountable than they really are. It's easy to get stuck in a negative thought pattern where we focus only on how hard things are and how unfair the world is. When we're stuck in this mindset, it can be difficult to see a way out.

Obstacles can also make us feel as if we're not good enough. When we try and fail, it's easy to start questioning our abilities and worth as human beings. We may begin to believe that we're just not cut out for whatever we're trying to do or that we're not smart or talented enough to succeed. When these thoughts take hold, it can be tough to shake them off.

Obstacles can also take a toll on us by creating a sense of hopelessness. When we're faced with a big, scary obstacle, it's easy to feel defeated. We may begin to believe that there's no point in trying or that too much effort is required to overcome the obstacle. When we give up hope, we give up the possibility of success. With the right mindset and attitude, obstacles can be a positive force in our lives.

Obstacles can make us stronger. When we face challenges and overcome them, we build up our resilience muscles. We learn that we can handle more than we thought we could and that failing to overcome an obstacle once is not the same as failing to overcome it forever. We develop a sense of integrity and fortitude that can carry us through even the toughest times. We develop a sense of accomplishment.

The next time you're faced with an obstacle, try to approach it with a growth mindset. Consider it an opportunity for learning and growth rather than a roadblock in your way.

Life is full of unexpected twists and turns, and obstacles are just lessons you will encounter on your path to success. It's easy to get bogged down by negative emotions, but the key is to maintain a positive mindset.

Whether you're dealing with work-related issues, relationship problems, family drama, or other stressful situations, sometimes you have to stop and say, "Not today, Satan. Not today."

I've used this phrase many times. When you're at your wit's end and about to snap, use this phrase as a reminder that you will not give in. You will overcome this obstacle, and you will not accept defeat. You must believe that!

For many people, hitting a wall feels like failure. You might quit altogether or turn toward another direction. Sometimes, obstacles direct you to a new path, and knowing how to overcome them makes the difference between throwing in the towel or thriving.

When you feel overwhelmed by obstacles, slow down, and put these tips into practice.

1. Manage Your Emotions

Managing your emotions is crucial when overcoming obstacles. It's important to take a step back and analyze a situation before reacting impulsively. When I worked at NASA, I learned that our engineers, scientists, and astronauts are trained to control their emotions, especially during high-stress situations.

These professionals learned how to take a step back, analyze a situation, and find a way forward, no matter how bad the circumstances. They knew that when things went wrong, it was crucial that they stay calm and find a way forward.

When we face obstacles, it's important to let go of set expectations and focus on making the most of a tough situation.

2. Let Go and Let Flow: Maintain a Positive Mindset

A positive mindset is critical for overcoming obstacles. When you have a positive attitude, you become more confident in your ability to tackle challenges. A positive mindset also helps you stay open to new possibilities and ways of dealing with problems.

For example, if you are fired, maybe it's time to start a new career or your own business. If your partner betrays your trust, you can learn from this experience, and you may want to take it slower in your next relationship or look for red flags you might have missed the first time. A positive mindset allows you to revise your expectations and pivot to a new plan when necessary.

3. *Reframe Your Thinking and View Your Obstacles as Opportunities*

The way you think about obstacles can significantly affect how you approach them. Instead of seeing them as roadblocks, try to reframe them as opportunities for growth and learning. When you encounter an obstacle, ask yourself, "What can I learn from this experience?" Shifting your perspective can make you more likely to stay positive and motivated.

Treating obstacles as opportunities is another way to stay positive when faced with a challenge. Instead of focusing on the negative aspects of the situation, think about how you can use the obstacle to make yourself stronger, wiser, and better.

Ask yourself, "What are my strengths in this situation?" and, "What can I do right now to move forward?"

Research shows that how you deal with disappointment accurately predicts your ability to succeed. For example, if you shut down every time you face a roadblock or setback, you are less likely to succeed than if you refuse to accept defeat (APA, 2019).

Overcoming obstacles isn't easy, but like anything else, the only way to improve is to practice, practice, practice. When overcoming obstacles, setbacks, or disappointments, we must remember that even if we don't achieve our goals—or if doing so takes longer than expected— trying makes us better than we were before.

Throughout life, when you expect a good outcome, you'll often hit an obstacle and then find that you have to create a new plan.

Learn how to adapt masterfully to life's curveballs, but also understand that you're never entirely in control. Know that circumstances can and often will change.

Sometimes we must stop and say, "Not today, Satan," and remember that we are not alone in experiencing obstacles and setbacks.

Although we are not in control of whether setbacks will occur, we are completely in control of how we react to them and whether we accept defeat. Be kind to yourself in challenging moments. Retake control of your reactions and keep moving forward. Whether it's for a personal goal you've set for yourself or a challenge that's unexpectedly been thrown your way, obstacles can seem overwhelming. However, with the right mindset and approach, you can stay positive and overcome them.

The way you think about obstacles can significantly affect how you approach them. Instead of seeing them as roadblocks, try to reframe them as opportunities for growth and learning. When you encounter an obstacle, ask yourself, "What can I learn from this experience?"

Shifting your perspective can make you more likely to stay positive and motivated.

4. *Take Care of Yourself*

Obstacles can be stressful and draining, so it's important to prioritize self-care during these times. This may entail getting enough sleep, eating healthy, staying active, or just taking time to relax and recharge. When you take care of yourself, you'll be better equipped to handle the challenges that come your way.

5. *Find an Ally*

Facing obstacles alone can be daunting—seek support from friends, family, or a trusted professional. Talking through your challenges with someone you trust can help you gain perspective and find new solutions. Plus, having someone in your corner can be motivating and uplifting.

6. *Break It Down*

Sometimes obstacles can feel overwhelming because they seem too big to tackle all at once. Try breaking down a challenge you face into small, manageable steps. Focus on completing one step at a time and celebrate your progress along the way. This will help you stay motivated and see that progress is possible, even in the face of adversity.

7. *Focus on the Now*

When facing obstacles, it's easy to get caught up in what might happen in the future or what has happened in the past. However, staying in the present moment can help you stay positive and focused.

Take things one day at a time and try to find joy and meaning. By focusing on what you can do right now, you'll feel more empowered and motivated.

8. *Celebrate Small Wins*

It is important to celebrate small wins along the way. When facing obstacles, progress can sometimes feel slow or even nonexistent. However, by focusing on the small victories, no matter how small they may be, you'll be more likely to stay positive and motivated.

Whether it's completing a small task, overcoming a minor setback, or simply staying focused on your goals, take time to acknowledge how far you have already come.

Final Thoughts

To recap, we learned that obstacles are a part of your journey, not the end of it. They can be challenges to overcome, opportunities to grow, and stepping stones to success.

Remember, managing your emotions, having a positive mindset, and looking at obstacles as opportunities are the keys to staying positive when facing roadblocks. Next time you encounter an obstacle, take a deep breath, say, "Not today, Satan," and use these tips to overcome it.

You and only you have the power to control how you react to challenges and setbacks.

Stay positive, stay motivated, and keep moving forward. The road may not always be easy, but with the right mindset, you can conquer any obstacle that comes your way!

Chapter Four

Change

"Yesterday, I was clever, so I wanted to change the world. Today I am wise, so I am changing myself."

— *Rumi*

Spring is one of my favorite times of the year. It's a season that marks a fresh and new beginning—a time of change. Spring is the time for making plans, completing projects, and experiencing changes in our daily lives.

As humans, we are almost constantly in a state of flux, from the subtle happenings of every minute of every day to grander life transitions. Change can be overwhelming—whether it involves losing a job, changing careers, ending a relationship, losing a loved one, or experiencing any other unexpected situation. I'm sure you have been through many changes throughout your life—you may even be experiencing one right now.

Change is unavoidable, and it can be challenging to navigate. Life is full of twists and turns, so we must learn to adapt and grow through them all.

I've experienced my fair share of change. As someone who coaches from a wheelchair, I've had to adapt to physical limitations and find new ways to approach challenges. But I've also experienced other changes that have forced me to push myself out of my comfort zone, such as starting my own business, developing peer coaching relationships, retiring early, and moving to a state where the cold weather affects my MD.

I understand the struggle all too well. I know the fear and resistance that can come with change. When I was diagnosed with MD, my life turned upside down. Everything became different. I was used to a specific routine, and it wasn't easy to imagine doing anything differently.

I went from running, to walking with a cane or walker, to using a wheelchair. The thought of making these changes over time was unnerving, and the fear of the unknown was tremendous, creating an inertia that kept me from progressing toward my goals.

I quickly realized that I had to embrace change if I wanted to move forward. I had to be willing to try new things and take risks, recognizing that change can be exciting and empowering if we embrace it with a positive attitude. It wasn't easy, but it was necessary for my personal and professional growth.

Many people don't like change at all—they want their world to stay the same, and they refuse to adapt. They may accept change after 10 years but won't do anything about that change for another 15 or 20 years.

This resistance is natural because it's our brain's way of protecting us from the unknown. However, it's important to remember that the unknown is not always a bad thing: it can lead to some of the most significant opportunities in our lives.

How Do We Overcome the Fear of Change?

You can manage this process by focusing on what you want to change; what you can do to make this change happen; and which aspects of change, if any, you can control.

Are you afraid of failure? Are you worried about what others will think?

Once you identify these fears, you can work on addressing them and finding solutions to move forward.

It's easy to get caught up in uncertainty and doubt when faced with new circumstances. So, I've listed three simple tips for approaching and managing change.

1. Acceptance

It's happened—it's here. Name it and claim it. It's important to acknowledge and accept that change is happening and that it may be outside your control. This can be difficult because it often requires us to let go of the past and embrace the unknown.

To adapt to change, we must tweak our mindset. If we approach it with resistance, we may hold ourselves back from growth and new opportunities. If we embrace change with a positive attitude and a willingness to learn, we can be ready for the possibilities that await us. Ask yourself: what happened? How do I overcome this situation and move forward? How do I avoid making this mistake again? Is this something I can adapt to?

Once we accept that change is inevitable, we can begin to shift our mindset and focus on what we *can* control.

2. Control What You Can

If something is out of your control, move past it. Shifting your focus to the areas you can change is critical to moving forward and achieving peace of mind.

We may not be able to control external circumstances, but we can control our reaction to them.

Ask yourself whether there is anything you can make peace with or let go of. When you identify these things, you can begin to move forward. Progress may require taking steps to improve your skills or knowledge, seek support from others, or simply focus on your well-being.

3. Devise an Action Plan

Focus on those areas critical to reaching a positive outcome. This involves setting clear goals and identifying the steps necessary to achieve them. When you break down your goals into smaller achievable tasks, measurable progress toward your objectives will become easier. This can help you build confidence and momentum, making it easier to tackle more significant challenges down the road.

It's also important to be flexible and willing to adjust your plans as you go, given that unexpected challenges and opportunities may arise.

This process can help reduce change-related stress and anxiety. By accepting that change is inevitable and focusing on what you can control, you can feel more empowered and less overwhelmed by your circumstances.

Change is necessary for growth. As difficult as it may be, it's important to push through feelings of fear and resistance. Without change, we may become stagnant and complacent, missing out on new opportunities and experiences that can enrich our lives and help us become better versions of ourselves.

In light of this, here are a few strategies to help embrace the changes that come your way:

1. Take a "What's in It for Me?" Approach

View change as an opportunity rather than a threat. This will help you approach new situations with a positive attitude and a willingness to adapt. Focus on the positive outcomes, envisioning the benefits change can bring rather than dwelling on its potentially negative consequences.

2. *Seek Support*

It is important to remember that making changes doesn't mean you have to do it alone. Seek support from a mentor, trusted friend, or professional coach for inspiration and guidance—people who have successfully adapted to change and can help you stay accountable while you navigate the challenges that come with change. Talking through fears and concerns with someone you trust can help alleviate feelings of anxiety and uncertainty.

It can also be helpful to seek resources and information throughout the whole process. Whether this includes reading self- help books, attending workshops or seminars, or seeking out online resources, there are many tools available to help you navigate change.

3. *Engage in Self-Care*

When dealing with any change, self-care is key. Change can be stressful on the body and mind. As new situations arise, you may find that previous methods of dealing with change are no longer effective. Taking care of yourself will help you to better manage the thoughts and feelings you experience while working through challenging transitions. It is never selfish to prioritize yourself—especially during times of change.

4. *Be Real With Yourself*

One important key to embracing change is setting realistic expectations about how you feel and what you can accomplish. Any time you're dealing with change, you will encounter setbacks, which can be disappointing and frustrating. You might make a mistake or face an intimidating obstacle that you don't know how to tackle. Don't compare yourself to others. Accept that everyone is different and has different circumstances, and don't put pressure on yourself to be perfect. This is impossible! Aim for progress, not perfection.

Learn from your mistakes and use them as an opportunity so that you can do better next time. It can be hard to let go of how you think everything should be done and accept a situation for what it is. If you do, it will help you find balance and live a more fulfilling life. Ultimately, the secret to creating successful changes in our lives is focusing on our goals, remaining patient with ourselves, and staying motivated even when faced with setbacks. It's important to remember that change is not a one-time event but a continuous process of growth and evolution.

Final Thoughts

Let's be honest. Even with all these tips and tricks, change can be a real pain in the neck. It can be messy, uncomfortable, and downright frustrating.

But whether it involves personal growth, new experiences, or a fresh perspective on life, change can be the catalyst for truly amazing things.

Let's embrace the change that comes our way, remember what we can control, and accept the ever-flowing river of life.

Go forth and conquer the world, my friends, and may the winds of change be ever in your favor!

Chapter Five

Learn Something New

"Always walk through life as if you have something new to learn, and you will."

— *Vernon Howard*

Learning is a lifelong process we all engage in, whether we realize it or not. We learn new skills from childhood to adulthood. We have a natural drive to explore, learn, and grow, which encourages us to improve our quality of life and self-worth by focusing on the ideas and goals that inspire us.

Learning allows us to pursue personal interests and passions and achieve personal development. Personal development means different things to different people. It might mean pursuing a hobby or passion, learning a new skill, or taking on a new challenge. One of the great things about learning is that it is not limited to a certain age or confined to a formal educational environment. Lifelong learning can happen anywhere and at any time—it can be formal or informal, structured or unstructured. It may come from reading books, taking courses, engaging in conversations, or simply observing the world around us. It allows us to embrace the fact that we are all capable of change, growth, and redirection at any time. We do not have to pick a path straight out of the womb and follow it.

It's also important to remember that learning is a personal journey. Whether we are deconstructing past experiences or absorbing new knowledge, we must approach learning with an open mind and a willingness to explore new ideas. We have the power to decide what our learning experience looks like. We decide what to learn, how to learn, and from whom we will learn.

As a lifelong learner myself, I would like to share some of the many benefits of learning new things, which I have outlined below.

1. It Lights a Fire Under Your Butt

Lifelong learning brings renewed self-motivation and helps you recognize your interests and goals by reigniting your spark as an individual—reducing boredom, making life interesting, and presenting future opportunities. By figuring out what inspires you, you can regain control and be reminded that you can do what you want. This renewed sense of motivation can give you a boost in all areas of life. You never know where your interests will lead you, but by focusing on them, you can uncover new paths and experiences you never thought possible.

2. It Unlocks Your Soft Skills

Learning new things can improve your personal and professional skills. This can also help you build or reinforce important soft skills, such as goal setting, self-discipline, creativity, critical thinking, time management, problem-solving, and adaptability, all of which can improve your personal and professional life.

Given all the times I have gone trick or treating on Halloween, I have likely uttered some rendition of the words "Trick or treat!" more than a thousand times. Surprisingly, this seemingly innocent event of dressing up and collecting sweets can teach us valuable lessons about the soft skills needed to succeed.

When you are trick or treating, you are developing social skills and building confidence whether or not you are aware of it. Not everyone can strut out the door with their faces painted like a puppy, wearing blood-spattered robes, or displaying glittering butterfly wings, then go and knock on strangers' doors.

Striking up conversations with strangers and chatting with neighbors while approaching them for candy can make one anxious. However, trick or treating exposes children to a social process that helps them gain confidence, build self-esteem, and improve their emotional well-being. No matter how shy or nervous you were as a child, the lesson was clear: a little smile and three small words can go a long way in boosting emotional well-being. Of course, a bonanza of candy was enough to encourage you to dig deep and put on the best show possible.

Another important lesson from Halloween is that creativity can give you an edge over others. Trick or treating taught us the value of standing out because the more creative the costume, the better the chance of getting a pile of candy. We all knew the costume all-stars in our neighborhoods who had winning smiles and personalities and who carved elaborate pumpkins to display on the porch every year. It's important to remember that creativity is for everyone, and the challenge lies in believing in ourselves and coming up with novel yet distinct ideas. As children, we knew that if we made people laugh or smile, we were sure to hit a candy gold mine.

Knowing your audience is also a crucial skill, and trick or treating can help teach such a skill. As we approached each house as children, we'd be as sweet as possible or play into our characters to gain an extra handful of candy. Understanding and leveraging your audience's expectations is central to making your pitch convincing and relevant.

Finally, learning when to walk away is another skill that we can take away. Trick or treating teaches us to skip the decoration- deprived houses with the lights off, and the same applies to life. Recognizing the subtle (or not-so-subtle) hints that it's time to walk away from a bad situation is a valuable skill. Whether it's a job, relationship, or friendship, we should walk away from things that no longer positively contribute to our lives.

When Halloween approaches, watch the trick or treaters run around your neighborhood. Children's eager faces and excited laughter have something to teach us. Halloween is not just about candy and costumes: it's also about the unwritten lessons that can provide a lifetime's worth of valuable insights.

3. *It Boosts Your Self-Confidence*

Becoming more knowledgeable increases your communication skills and self-confidence in your personal and professional life.

Lifelong learning helps you improve your communication skills, such as active listening, empathy, and conflict resolution. These skills enhance our relationships, improve our leadership abilities, and increase our overall success in life.

Self-confidence stems from the satisfaction of devoting time and effort to learning, improving, and promoting a sense of accomplishment at the end of the process. Learning new things can help you discover new interests and passions or even challenge long- held beliefs and assumptions. As you pursue lifelong learning, you may develop a deeper understanding of yourself, your values, and the world around you, leading to greater personal fulfillment and a sense of purpose.

In our professional lives, self-confidence involves acquiring trust in our knowledge and our ability to apply it. Lifelong learning opens new career opportunities. It's not about keeping an old job but rather about exploring new roles and careers. For example, if your current job does not suit you, you might consider taking an online course that offers a valuable certification in your preferred field. In some cases, a career transition may even be possible without the need to go back to school.

4. *It Boosts Your Brain Power*

Studies have shown that lifelong learning helps improve mental, physical, and cognitive health. More neural pathways are formed when neurons in the brain are stimulated, and the more pathways that form, the faster the impulses can travel. Better cognitive function, longer attention span, stronger memory, improved reasoning skills, and reduced risk of dementia are just a few merits of learning (Simone & Scuilli, 2006).

For example, cooking is a learned skill that improves your cognition and fine motor skills. Cooking trains your brain to handle various challenges, such as measuring portions, balancing temperatures, and multitasking. It helps you keep your neural pathways active and gain new experiences—especially with that new hot dish (a hot dish is a term people in the Midwest often use for a prepared casserole) recipe you're dying to try. All these factors contribute to our health and well-being.

How and Where Do I Start Learning New Things?

There are many ways to learn, and each person's approach may vary depending on their interests, learning styles, and resources. However, a few key fundamental approaches are helpful for those looking to expand their knowledge and skill set. A reliable way to learn new things is through reading, which exposes us to new ideas and perspectives. A person can read books, articles, blogs, or research papers in their area of interest to gain a deeper understanding of the subject matter and learn from the experiences and insights of others.

With the rise of video-sharing platforms such as YouTube and Vimeo, there is no shortage of educational content available online. Anyone can watch videos and documentaries on various topics— from science and history to philosophy and psychology—and learn from experts about complex concepts. Reading and watching educational content not only helps us acquire new knowledge but also help improve our vocabulary, critical-thinking skills, and writing abilities.

We can also learn new things by attending workshops, classes, or conferences. Educational events provide opportunities to learn from field experts and interact with like-minded individuals. The most valuable way to learn is through experience. There is no substitute for hands-on learning; the lessons we learn from experience are often some of the most profound and impactful. Joining a professional organization or community can provide you with access to resources, support, and mentorship from experienced mentors and peers.

Curiosity and openness will fuel your lifelong learning. Talk to strangers. Be present in conversations. Seek out ideas that stimulate your interest. Keep the sense of wonder you developed as a child that sparked inquiry and continual exploration. Whether through volunteering, interning, or simply trying new things, taking action and learning from our successes and failures are critical components of personal growth.

"Upskilling" and "Reskilling" Are Not Just Buzzwords

Not long ago, people relied on a degree, diploma, or certificate to enter the workforce and thereafter continued in the same job for decades. Today, technology has disrupted every industry, creating new professions, rendering others obsolete, and forcing employees to upskill and reskill quickly and regularly. Upskilling means advancing and improving on a skill set that you already possess. Reskilling means developing a new skill set in preparation for different opportunities.

According to Harvard Business Publishing, 54% of the workforce will require upskilling or reskilling by 2025. A total of 85% of employees surveyed acknowledged that they have a skill gap, but only 41% thought their managers understood their shortcomings. Additionally, PricewaterhouseCoopers International Limited's 22nd Annual Global CEO Survey (2019) revealed that skill shortages threaten companies' growth, which in turn stunts innovation, limits the pursuit of market opportunities, and jeopardizes business quality.

Learning from mentors or coaches is a superlative way to gain new knowledge and skills. An expert who provides guidance, support, and encouragement can be essential to our learning, helping us identify our strengths and weaknesses and providing us with the tools we need to reach our goals.

Sometimes, the best way to learn is simply by taking action. Taking on new challenges and experiences can push you out of your comfort zone and provide opportunities for growth. Whether you decide to learn a new language, try a new sport, or travel to a new country, the possibilities for learning are endless. Whether you want to study a new language, pick up a skill, or learn a new subject, a strong foundation is key. Once you master basic skills, you will learn advanced concepts and material faster.

Here are some tips to help build a strong foundation of new knowledge:

1. Search for Different Sources

When a topic is difficult to understand, you can improve your comprehension by finding other sources to learn from. Utilize multiple sources to access alternative teaching styles and perspectives.

2. Use a Simple Memory Trick

Learning may require memorization. An easy and effective way to remember multiple things is to create a visual link from one item to another through a story. For instance, let's say you wanted to learn the seven largest cities in the United States: New York, Los Angeles,

Chicago, Houston, Phoenix, Philadelphia, and San Antonio. The next step would be to choose a memorable image or story for each city, then link the first to the second, the second to the third, and so on. This simple memory technique is a powerful way to recall multiple steps and extensive material.

3. Teach Someone Else

One of the most powerful ways to learn is to teach someone else. As you teach someone a concept, you are compelled to break it down, allowing yourself to understand it more clearly. Teaching others is an exciting, rewarding way to learn something new and help others learn, too. Answering questions that someone else has about the topic is also an easy way to test your knowledge and take stock of what you don't know. Teaching constantly helps you to refine your knowledge.

Are you ready to begin your journey toward growth and personal development? Before starting, you must be willing to let go of old beliefs that no longer serve you. It is rather easy to attach a sense of pride to our existing beliefs, even if they do not necessarily align with our current lifestyle. This is the only way you can begin your personal development.

As John Delony, author of *Own Your Past Change Your Future: A Not-So-Complicated Approach to Relationships, Mental Health & Wellness*, has reminded us, clinging to certainty is like an addiction that can cause anxiety. It slows our personal development. But the situation is different for open-minded people.

Open-minded people are intellectually curious, creative, and imaginative, as Frieda Birnbaum, a research psychologist and psychotherapist in Saddle River, New Jersey, has noted. Open- minded people tend to see things that others may not, and their willingness to be honest can lead to amazing things. These individuals are trailblazers in personal growth and development.

Reframing a negative mindset in reaction to new ideas is crucial to embracing change and personal growth. Stephen McGarvey, the author of *Ignite a Shift: Engaging Minds, Guiding Emotions, and Driving Behavior*, suggests that changing your mind requires evaluating your thinking, emotional state, and indeed the change itself. It is important to ask yourself questions that guide your brain toward a strategy for change. Without change, there is no personal growth.

Positive self-talk is another powerful tool for personal growth— but it's not enough on its own. You must use language that engages and guides your brain toward new possibilities. As McGarvey explains, defining a well-formed outcome and using your brain effectively to achieve your goal is fundamental to personal development.

Another way to embrace personal growth is by taking a stance of emotional ambivalence, as Naomi Rothman, an associate professor at Lehigh University College of Business, suggests. By listening to new information with empathy, respect, and impartiality, you can be cognitively flexible, open-minded, and able to consider multiple perspectives better. Ambivalence increases one's motivation to consider positive and negative information before making important decisions.

When you were a child, you probably asked a lot of questions. To continue on the path of personal growth, keep that same curiosity and always ask why. Seek out counter-opinions and alternative viewpoints. Be open to changing your mind; it will allow you to learn and push yourself further.

Another way to continue your personal growth is through lifelong learning. Lifelong learners realize that learning does not stop when school ends. Never stop seeking opportunities to learn and at the core of every learning process lie two fundamental concepts: deep learning and surface learning. Deep learning is a committed approach to learning where the learner applies critical thinking skills to devise a solution to a posed problem. Whereas the surface learning approach involves the learner only being willing to scrape the surface of the material being studied and concentrating only on the required portions without getting into the details.

Constructive criticism will also help in your growth. Be proactive about asking for feedback from mentors, peers, and coaches. A community of supporters can help you solve problems, identify opportunities, and fuel your personal development. Frequent feedback will help you to grow continually, both personally and professionally. Developing deep knowledge in multiple areas with cross-disciplinary awareness makes uncovering unexpected connections and convergences easier, while being an expert in a topic requires continuous education.

Learn to trust the process and prioritize it over goals. When you prioritize the process of learning, you open yourself to new opportunities. Changing your mindset gives you the flexibility to follow your curiosity, which may lead you to opportunities you would not have discovered otherwise. Give yourself the gift of grace. It's okay if you don't know something—embrace this lack of knowledge as a challenge and an opportunity to learn something new. Remember to take breaks and always prioritize self-care.

Final Thoughts

As I reflect on my journey of learning and self-improvement, I am struck by the power of pursuing new knowledge and skills. Whether you are seeking to master a new language, explore a new hobby, or advance your career, there is no limit to what you can achieve when you commit to lifelong learning.

I leave you with this thought: never underestimate the value of investing in yourself.

With every new skill you acquire, every new idea you explore, and every new challenge you overcome, you are building a brighter, more fulfilling future for yourself and those around you. Go forth with confidence and enthusiasm, and never stop learning and growing. Remember that the path to personal growth is not always easy, but it is always worth it.

As Aristotle said, "The roots of education are bitter, but the fruit is sweet."

Welcome the challenges, celebrate the successes, and, above all, never give up on the potential that lies within you.

You have the power to achieve great things; you just need to believe in yourself!

Chapter Six

Comfort Zone

"You never change your life until you step out of your comfort zone; change begins at the end of your comfort zone."

— *Roy T. Bennett*

As a culture, we are obsessed with being comfortable. We will spend great amounts of money, time, and energy to maintain our current level of comfort or to move into an even comfier state of mind—a place of ease and pleasure. As a disabled veteran who uses a wheelchair, stepping outside my comfort zone involves more than just confidence. There are many additional factors I have to think about. In my daily routine, to do the things that are necessary, I must become aware of the tasks I struggle with and what I feel comfortable doing.

These tasks, such as transferring myself from a bed to a wheelchair or transferring myself from a wheelchair to a toilet or shower chair, may be simple to others, but they can be difficult for me. Preparing a meal, for example, or attempting to cut my own food can be difficult to manage when I feel fatigued.

From time to time, challenging myself and stepping outside my comfort zone can be a good thing, even when that means doing things I might find difficult because of my disability, such as driving my hand-controlled technology SUV, writing articles for my hometown newspaper, or even writing this book.

Typing has become increasingly difficult and time-consuming for me, but through technology, I use speak-and-type software to accommodate my struggles. This is something I am getting better at over the years. Trying new things can be a challenge for various reasons— the first being confidence. This is something that applies to everyone: trying to do a task you don't feel confident about isn't always easy.

Close your eyes for a moment and imagine yourself in a cozy bubble. This bubble represents your comfort zone, a place where familiarity and routine provide you with a sense of safety and security. It's where you feel comfortable, where the known and the predictable reign supreme. Living life in your comfort zone has obvious benefits: low stress, reduced anxiety, and general feelings of well-being. But it can also feel predictable, making you feel like you're in a holding pattern. Sometimes, this cozy bubble won't fulfill your need for growth and new experiences.

However, too much uncertainty can lead to anxiety and a lack of productivity. Moving out of your comfort zone in consistent positive ways can allow you to strike the right balance between certainty and uncertainty. Outside of the cozy bubble lies a world filled with endless opportunities for growth, fulfillment, and personal transformation. To get there, consider the following four things:

1. *Embrace the Unknown*

Have you ever noticed that some of life's most memorable and fulfilling moments happen when you summon the courage to venture into the unknown? Picture yourself starting a conversation with a stranger, taking up a new hobby, or pursuing a career change that fills you with nervousness and excitement. These moments are the catalysts for personal growth and transformation.

When you step outside your comfort zone, you open yourself up to a world of new experiences, perspectives, and opportunities. You challenge the limits of what you thought possible and expand the horizons of your potential. It is through these experiences that you will uncover hidden strengths, untapped talents, and a wellspring of resilience you never knew resided within you.

2. *See the Possibilities and Welcome the Growth*

Beyond the confines of your comfort zone lies a world brimming with infinite possibilities—a realm where dreams take flight and extraordinary achievements are born. When you dare to venture into this realm, you shatter your self-imposed limitations and tap into your full potential.

When you embrace the unknown, you unlock doors that lead to new connections, opportunities, and experiences you could never have imagined. You find yourself in the company of like-minded individuals, united by a shared passion for growth and exploration. The universe conspires in your favor, aligning circumstances to support your journey.

Think back to a time when you faced a daunting challenge or pursued a goal that initially seemed out of reach. Remember the doubts, fears, and that nagging voice inside your head questioning your abilities?

Now, reflect on how you felt when you pushed through those self-imposed limitations, exceeded your own expectations, and emerged on the other side stronger and more empowered than ever.

Stepping outside your comfort zone is an invitation to grow, evolve, and become the best version of yourself. It is a testament to your courage, resilience, and unwavering determination. When you willingly embrace discomfort and uncertainty, you embark on a personal growth journey that transcends the boundaries of your current reality. The most successful people in the world have a deep need for growth that pushes them to leave their comfort zone in search of new things.

Just beyond your comfort zone is a space where a growth mindset takes over, and you realize you can be at ease while stretching and growing. Each step forward, no matter how small, propels you closer to realizing your dreams and aspirations.

3. *Manage the Discomfort*

Think back to the last time you felt so uncomfortable and uneasy that your heart raced and your stomach churned. Remember how it felt?

Recognizing these physical sensations is key to understanding when you're actually stepping outside your comfort zone. By acknowledging the discomfort, you can embrace it as a sign of growth rather than a reason to retreat.

Almost everyone, even the most adventurous among us, has some version of a comfort zone. Maybe you always follow the same routine at the gym, or you gravitate toward a certain type of person when dating. Alternatively, maybe you've been employed at the same job for ages, and the mere thought of quitting and doing something else is enough to make you break out in a cold sweat. Whatever it is, a comfort zone feels safe, but it can be limiting and keep you from seizing opportunities for growth. When you leave your comfort zone, keep in mind that feelings of fear don't have to equate to being in the panic zone. Fear can, and often does, live alongside learning and growth.

As a coach, I continually push my clients to explore the unfamiliar, whether that means reaching out to new professional contacts, starting a passion project they've been putting off, or simply taking a small yet scary step toward achieving their goals.

However, it can often be difficult to change one's mindset about risk and reward, especially if one takes refuge in familiarity. When was the last time you felt uncomfortable? What did it feel like? Where did you feel it in your body? Was it in your chest? Your stomach?

Understanding how discomfort manifests in your body can make it easier to notice when you are out of your comfort zone. It allows you to put yourself in situations that make you uncomfortable but open you up to growth. To that end, stepping out of your comfort zone—at least occasionally—can be a worthy endeavor.

Below, I would like to share some tips using the acronym *HARPO*—which stands for "have," "acknowledge," "research," "pick," and "own"—that can make stepping out of your comfort zone easier.

Have a compelling reason for stepping out of your comfort zone. Without strong motivation, it can be challenging to break free from the familiar. Take the time to envision what it would be like to take that step and immerse yourself in that new vision, idea, or thought. Allow it to build a powerful momentum that propels you into action.

Acknowledge the inherent scariness of the unknown and challenge yourself to break out of your comfort zone. By immersing yourself in new experiences, you shock your system into becoming comfortable with the unfamiliar. As you push your boundaries, you will become so engrossed in the process that fear eventually loses its grip on you.

Research information to educate yourself. Your goal here is to learn more about the skill or activity you're pursuing. Seek advice from those who have walked similar paths, read books on the subject, and explore relevant articles on the internet. By arming yourself with knowledge, you will cultivate confidence and reduce fear of the unknown.

Pick activities that challenge you. Make a list and mark the item you want to start with. Putting your aspirations into writing will help you formulate a plan that details how you will step outside your comfort zone. Instead of merely contemplating change, developing specific ideas will compel you to put those plans into motion. You'll notice corresponding changes in your body and emotional state as your mindset shifts.

Own it! Tell yourself, "I am fearless!" Disempowering thought patterns often keep us trapped within our comfort zone. To break free, replace those thoughts with empowering ones. Adopt a new perspective and take inspired action. Repeating the mantra "I am fearless!" and envisioning yourself successfully conquering your fears can help reprogram your mind and propel you forward.

If you frequently find yourself regretting missed opportunities or sensing an internal push to act, it may be time to venture beyond your comfort zone. Think of your comfort zone as a place to stop and rest for a bit while you challenge yourself. It should not be where you remain forever. Nothing in nature stays the same forever. We can emerge outside of our comfort zone by choice or by force.

Final Thoughts

Pushing yourself past your comfort zone can be difficult. And it can be even more difficult when you do it on your own (especially if it's new for you). It is also difficult when you're surrounded by people who themselves are stuck or are trying to keep you in your comfort zone. All that is bad juju!

Bring the right influence into your life in the form of a coach or mentor who understands and pushes you outside your comfort zone. You wouldn't want to learn how to swim from someone who only knows the theory but can't actually swim.

Additionally, seek individuals and communities that are committed to growing and pushing themselves continually. A coach, mentor, or ambitious peer will guide you outside your comfort zone.

Every person faces this choice, knowingly or not. You can settle for what you know—the seemingly safe, familiar, and routine. Alternatively, you can become receptive to opportunities for growth, challenging your personal status quo and redefining what you're capable of. When this becomes a habit, the benefits to be reaped throughout life are plentiful, such as better managing change, creating new relationships, and increasing your self-awareness. Know that every change, every step outside your comfort zone, is shaping you into the person you are meant to become!

Chapter Seven

Being Self-Aware

"The curious paradox is that when I accept myself just as I am, then I can change."

— *Carl R. Rogers*

You cannot welcome growth until you welcome self- acceptance.

As a coach, my focus with my clients is on making them see their potential, which lies in helping them maximize their strengths, recognize opportunities for improvement, and set and work toward goals. One factor, however, remains constant in my approach: the importance of self-awareness as a baseline skill that can be used to help you progress and improve your personal and professional development. If you become aware of your*self*, including your strengths and weaknesses, you will have a clear idea of the effects you can have on others and how to change them, if necessary. Becoming more effective will only reap rewards in both your professional and personal life.

One helpful way to become more aware of the complete and total self is to divide it into four parts, namely: physical, emotional, mental, and spiritual.

1. Physical

Having an awareness of our body helps us interpret how we're feeling in a given moment and day to day regarding our overall wellness. Our bodily awareness is usually strong when we're experiencing great physical pain or distress. When we feel physically neutral or perhaps slightly positive or negative, we can block our awareness of the physical body and replace it with emotional awareness. The key is to stay in tune with ourselves and our bodies, which is a surefire way to navigate through life with a lot more enjoyment and success.

2. Emotional

In a culture that values logic and reason, emotions are often undervalued. When people become emotionally expressive, others may instinctively tell them to calm down or act rationally. Being emotional is often considered to be synonymous with being out of control.

This assumption might give you the idea that emotions are to be avoided, but such a position would be harmful. Emotions serve an important purpose in providing the self with information about the environment and what to avoid or embrace. Typically, when we speak of our bodies or our emotions, we speak in terms of feelings or sensations—external stimuli that come upon us rather than internal stimuli that we create. This gives the impression of passivity, which is where we are slaves to our physical and emotional needs rather than choosing how we feel and react to those feelings.

The most important thing to remember is that we cannot avoid our emotions, but we can intervene. Through our actions, we can change how we react to our current emotional state, which, in turn, can transform our future emotions. Being able to identify how you feel at any given moment is an important step toward becoming more self- aware.

3. Mental

The mental aspect of yourself concerns your thoughts and imagination. Like physical and emotional feelings, thoughts have the capacity to occur without your control. Yet it's much easier to change your thoughts consciously, especially when you practice being more aware of them. When we think, we often think in sentences or words, but just as often, we think in images or words and phrases that act as a kind of shorthand. It's like talking to yourself in your mind and visualizing what you might say before it comes out. In these moments, you are visualizing your self-awareness through the use of concrete, photograph-like mental images.

4. Spiritual

The spiritual self is about your continuing sense of identity. It encompasses your worldview and acts as a source of motivation. If the emotional and mental self are about the feelings and thoughts of a person in each moment, the spiritual self is about the interconnectedness of thoughts and feelings that form a sense of personal identity over time.

Having self-awareness allows you to evaluate and interpret your behaviors, emotions, and actions. I see self-awareness as a way for you to create what works for you so that you can design your lifestyle on your terms. Tasha Eurich (2018), a researcher and organizational psychologist, and her team of researchers came up with two ways self awareness can manifest itself, which I think are important to note: internal and external self-awareness. I see this cognizance as the gap between how we see ourselves and how others see us.

Internal self-awareness is how you perceive your own values, passions, and aspirations and how you fit with your environment. It involves understanding your reactions (including thoughts, feelings, and behaviors), your triggers, and your impact on others. Most people do not have a robust understanding of their own thoughts and emotions (although most think they do), leading to bad decisions that can hurt themselves and others.

For example, someone who finds themselves slipping into a bad habit again without understanding why, lacks internal self-awareness. This happens because they don't know themselves well enough to understand why they're continuing this habit, or at least enough to recognize the possibility that they are in fact in control. A lack of internal self-awareness can manifest itself as manipulation— managing others by controlling them with fear or guilt. This is because people who lack internal awareness do not know what it is that will make them feel good about themselves, and they may seek it through other means. Bringing awareness of your feelings to yourself at any given moment allows you to understand yourself and your environment better, both in the moment and after it has passed.

External self-awareness is the ability to understand the external factors that influence you. External self-awareness creates an atmosphere wherein people become more understanding of one another by recognizing the differences, as well as the similarities, among us all. We often refer to this skill as the ability to "read the room." If you understand how others see you, then you are more likely to demonstrate empathy toward others. Knowing how to read between the lines and pick up on social cues is a critical skill. Many of us have been in a meeting where someone gets upset and the mood shifts. Someone who is externally aware will feel the energy changing in the room and may attempt to diffuse the situation.

The goal of self-awareness is to strike a balance between your internal and external self-awareness—or to see yourself as others see you. When these perceptions match, you can target areas for improvement and change how you interact with yourself and with others.

The Importance of Self-Awareness

Developing self-awareness is important because it allows people to assess their growth and effectiveness and change course when necessary. Even though most people think they are self-aware, they are not. However, self-awareness is a skill we can learn to improve. Someone who is not self-aware may encounter obstacles—or the same one repeatedly—and not understand why they do so. Someone who is self-aware will examine themselves honestly to get to the root of their problem. Despite encountering the same problems, a self-aware individual becomes well-equipped to deal with these obstacles.

Maybe people think you talk too much. A person who is not self-aware may get frustrated or perhaps fail to notice that people are annoyed by them. A self-aware person, however, will examine the facts and accept flaws in their social skills, recognizing that perhaps they do not listen enough to others or are not fully engaged in the present conversation.

A vital way of becoming more effective in both your personal and professional life is by increasing your self-awareness. If you can and do become aware of yourself, including your strengths and weaknesses, you will have a much better idea of your effects on others and how to change them, if necessary.

Self-awareness is about paying attention. It is your internal consciousness actively gathering and processing information from within. It is how you experience life.

The Eurich group (2018) researched the nature of self- awareness, finding that people with greater self-awareness are happier and have better relationships. They experience a greater sense of personal and social control as well as higher levels of job satisfaction than those who lack self-awareness.

When we look outward, we understand how people view us and are more likely to be empathetic toward those with different perspectives. People whose self-perception matches others' perceptions of them are more likely to empower, include, and recognize others.

1. The Dangers of Lacking Self-Awareness

It is critical to understand the dangers associated with a lack of self-awareness, from missed opportunities to strained relationships. Without self-awareness, you may not recognize your own strengths and weaknesses.

A lack of self-awareness can also make it difficult to recognize when you are in a toxic situation, such as an abusive relationship or a dead-end job. When you lack self-awareness, it may seem as if you are trying to navigate through life without a GPS, finding yourself lost at every turn. What's more, don't even think about trying to give someone else directions when you can't even make it three blocks from where you started!

We must recognize the signs that indicate we are not fully attuned to our inner selves—the guideposts that are leading us toward a path of personal transformation. Recognizing your self-awareness (or lack thereof) can seem challenging or nearly impossible if you don't even know what's wrong in the first place.

However, there are some telltale signs that indicate the hidden dangers of a lack of self-awareness.

1. Being Defensive

When we lack self-awareness, we tend to react impulsively without thoughtful consideration. We may find ourselves easily triggered by situations or people, leading to unnecessary conflict or strained relationships. Without understanding our own emotions, it may become challenging for us to communicate effectively and build healthy connections. Misunderstandings, conflicts, and a lack of trust can arise, causing damage to our personal and professional relationships. Reactive behavior prevents us from making conscious choices and often results in regrettable actions.

So, when a partner or friend calls out those instances—perhaps they said something unintentionally hurtful that triggered your emotions—the person lacking self-awareness tends to respond as if they are being attacked. That response may look like, "Oh, I was just trying to do X," or "I was just trying to help," rather than "I'm sorry, I overstepped my bounds." A lack of self-awareness can manifest as a tendency to blame others or external circumstances for our own shortcomings or failures. We may project our insecurities onto others, creating a distorted view of reality. This behavior hinders personal growth and prevents us from taking responsibility for our actions and their consequences.

2. *Inconsistent Behavior*

Without self-awareness, we might exhibit inconsistent behavior that is not aligned with our values or beliefs, creating confusion and instability. Inconsistency erodes trust, both in ourselves and in our relationships with others, and we may experience intense or confusing emotions without understanding why. Unresolved emotions can build up and negatively impact our mental and emotional well-being, leading to stress, anxiety, and depression.

3. *Lacking Empathy*

When we are not self-aware, it becomes challenging for us to empathize with others. We may become self-centered and unable to connect deeply with those around us. We are unaware of our emotions and often unable to see how our behaviors might be (negatively) contributing to a given situation. In these cases, we do not recognize our role in perpetuating the problem.

Unlike manipulative people, those who lack self-awareness are not deliberately hurtful. Individuals lacking self-awareness may have little inclination to engage in self-reflection, avoiding introspection and resisting questioning their beliefs and behaviors. Those who lack self-awareness have absolutely no idea of the chaos they may be creating around them.

4. Distracting Oneself From the Problem

We may avoid acknowledging our problems or challenges by engaging in distraction, transporting our minds to some other time, place, or world where we can be safe from the pain of day-to-day life. There is nothing wrong with distraction; we all need some sort of diversion every now and then to keep us sane and happy. The key is that we must be aware of our distractions and when we create them.

We stare at our phones, we obsess about the past or our potential futures, we make plans we will never keep, and we try to forget all the little challenges that arise in our path. It is important to note that lacking self-awareness is a common human experience—we all have our flaws. The key is to recognize these signs and actively work toward developing self-awareness. We must ensure that we are choosing when to divert our attention.

5. Wearing a Mask

We may wear a mask, or indeed several, to conceal our true emotions. This may be of economic necessity, wherein people feel the urge to conform to social pressures when their job depends on it. Masking can also be part of relationships, whereby people in unhealthy relationships engage in social camouflage to keep each other happy. When someone has been through verbal, emotional, or physical abuse, masking can feel like a survival mechanism. Another reason for masking is seeking social acceptance: someone may change their body language, tone of voice, or facial expressions around specific people or in certain situations. Whatever the case, a desire for acceptance usually lies at the root of most types of masking.

What masks do you wear? Who is behind your mask? Masks can be problematic when they become the norm and we lose ourselves in the process of trying to please others. We like some masks, but not others. We are forced to wear some masks to get along in life; others, we wear voluntarily and are afraid to remove them. Hiding your feelings can be temporarily liberating, but eventually, the mask will come off.

Learn to accept yourself and allow your authentic self to show up. Realize that even the most confident people occasionally wear masks, and it is in our human nature to desire acceptance. Achieving self-acceptance and awareness is a long journey, and you will have a much better chance of doing so if you are easy on yourself. It's exhausting to live an inauthentic life. Putting on a mask, or two, or ten, then taking a few off, then putting on a couple more, is exhausting! Worst of all, you may begin to forget who you really are.

Practical Strategies to Enhance Self-Awareness and Overcome Challenges

Self-awareness can be improved with effort. Those who invest the most effort will see their self-awareness increase quickly. Developing self-awareness is important for better relationships and a more fulfilling life, both in the workplace and at home. With an understanding of how we relate to others, we can adjust our behavior to interact with others more positively. By understanding what upsets us, we can improve our self-control. By understanding our weaknesses, we can learn how to manage them and reach our goals despite them.

Knowing more about yourself has many benefits. Self-awareness helps you become a better version of yourself, make the right decisions, and be confident in those decisions. There are several ways to become more self-aware:

1. Practice Mindfulness

Practicing mindfulness is a powerful tool for developing self-awareness. Do everything you can to be grateful for what you have in the moment, where you are in life, and who you are right now. This means focusing on the present without becoming overwhelmed or overly reactive to your circumstances.

This approach has many proven benefits, from reducing anxiety, depression, and chronic pain to improving sleep and reducing stress. When we pay attention to what is happening and to our experience of it, we can connect with others meaningfully. We heighten our senses and improve our decision-making, which enables us to move more safely and confidently through the world. A little self-awareness may be all we need to be present and create meaning out of the time we are given.

Mindfulness can also help us achieve goals such as weight loss or starting a new project. Mindfulness can help leaders stay centered on managing others and addressing external challenges effectively. Mindfulness is an important component in cultivating a happy, meaningful life. The more aware you are of how you are feeling, the more you will be able to find and maintain your center.

Our relationship with ourselves is the longest and most significant one we will ever have. But, although each of us will live in our own skin from birth to death, true self-awareness is something we must cultivate. Knowing ourselves will take some effort and practice, but it may be the most important thing we ever do.

2. Learn to Be Self-Reliant

You will never become self-aware if you do not learn to be self-reliant. The more independent you act, the more certain you will become of your own abilities. Self-reliance refers to the ability of an individual to rely on their own resources, skills, and judgment to meet their needs and navigate life's challenges. It enables you to develop self-knowledge and self-acceptance. It provides perspective, which can lead to greater direction in your life. Perhaps most importantly, it allows you to feel happy by yourself, about yourself, and for yourself, without relying on others to provide that happiness. Self-reliance does not mean living in a bubble without other people; it means knowing when to ask for help without sacrificing your sense of self.

So how can you best develop your self-reliance? Become aware of who you are and strive to become the best possible version of yourself. Here are some strategies that I believe can make that happen:

Think for Yourself. Be aware of your own thoughts, and do not allow them to take a back seat to the thoughts of others. Always look for ways to express your own creativity and think outside the box, even if in collaboration with others. Think critically about issues of importance to you without being unduly influenced by others, including news outlets and peers.

Know Yourself. Recognize your self-worth by naming and emphasizing your good traits. It is important to be aware of the good things you have accomplished. Look for opportunities to use your strengths and internal resources. Recount your accomplishments as a way to resist any temptation to give in to negative thoughts.

Learn for Yourself. Realistically assess your skill set to determine whether it is adequate to support your goals. You can hardly be self-reliant if you must depend on others to accomplish tasks that you should be doing yourself. Get whatever additional training you need. Keep abreast of your personal development opportunities. Look for ways to implement your new knowledge.

Balance Yourself. Practice self-care to replenish your creative energy and reduce stress. Manage your emotional and mental well- being by determining which emotions you feel at any point and whether you are triggered by others. Choose your own values and beliefs. Remember the "oxygen mask" effect: take care of yourself first so that you can then take care of others.

When you are self-reliant, you are responsible, and you empower yourself with great freedom.

3. Cultivate Empathy

Building empathy toward others can enhance your self- awareness. Take time to understand different perspectives and experiences. Engage in active listening and try to put yourself in someone else's shoes. Empathy will help you develop a broader understanding of human emotions and behaviors, including your own.

We often hear the phrase "perception is reality." This phrase is used to justify a perspective that may be objectively unjustifiable or just plain out of touch with reality. It is a defense mechanism to compel others to accept one's preferred so-called "reality." Although our perceptions feel real, it does not mean they should be used as a weapon against others.

We all live according to our perception of the reality we see and interpret through our personal filters, as determined by our beliefs, experiences, and values. This is natural. We must be aware of our perceptions and aim to remain open-minded, avoid misunderstanding others, and be nonjudgmental. This does not mean we must approve of others' points of view. Still, we should be open-minded and acknowledge different perceptions without judgment, allowing for increased opportunities for interpersonal communication. This approach assists coaches in helping clients find solutions to their challenges, take steps toward their goals, uncover gaps in their perception, and create the best possible outcomes.

The challenge we face is ensuring that our perceptions remain close to reality. Here are a few tips to keep in mind when managing your perceptions and those of others:

Do not assume that your perceptions are reality (they are just *your* reality).

Be respectful of others' perceptions (they might be right).

Recognize the distortions within you that may warp your perceptions. Seeing them will better ground your perceptions in reality rather than the other way around.

Seek validation from other credible people (don't just ask your friends because they likely have the same perceptions as you).

Be open-minded. Try opening the doors of perception. You will see that many possibilities exist beyond the ones that come immediately to mind. If you know what it is like to be judged unfairly, you may be able to look at others with a more open mind. You may find that when you take another look, things look different.

4. *Practice Emotional Awareness and Self-Reflection*

Developing emotional awareness is the gateway to self- awareness. Self-aware individuals understand and regulate their emotions effectively. These individuals are aligned with their emotional states and can recognize the impact their emotions have on their thoughts, behaviors, and relationships.

Self-aware individuals also have a deep understanding of their instincts and use them as a guide in decision-making. When we tap into our intuition, we access our inner wisdom and make choices aligned with our true selves. Developing emotional intelligence helps us face challenges more effectively and cultivate healthier connections with others. Pay attention to your emotions throughout the day and try to identify their triggers and underlying causes. Practice labeling your emotions and exploring how they influence your thoughts and actions.

Self-reflection is a hallmark of self-awareness. Those who engage in introspection regularly take time to examine their thoughts, beliefs, and behaviors. They question their assumptions, seek deep understanding, and learn from their experiences. Through self reflection, we gain insight into ourselves, paving the way for personal growth and self-improvement.

Take time to reflect on significant experiences and how they have shaped you. Consider your successes, failures, and lessons learned. Reflecting on your past allows you to gain insights into your values, motivations, and patterns of behavior.

Engage in regular self-reflection exercises to deepen your self-awareness. Set aside dedicated time to ask yourself meaningful questions: What are my core values and beliefs? What are my strengths and weaknesses? How do I behave in challenging situations? What triggers my emotional responses? How do I contribute to my relationships?

Write down your responses, and devise strategies for changing the things that bother you and improving those that bring joy to you and the people you care about. Keeping a journal can be an effective way to increase self-awareness. Write down your thoughts, feelings, and experiences regularly. Reflect on your entries and look for patterns, recurring themes, and triggers. Journaling can help you gain insight into your emotions and behaviors.

5. *Seek Help and Feedback*

Ask trusted friends, family members, or colleagues for honest feedback about your strengths and weaknesses. Be open to receiving constructive criticism and use it as an opportunity for growth. Feedback from others can provide valuable perspectives and highlight areas where you may lack self-awareness. If you find it challenging to enhance self-awareness on your own, consider seeking support from a therapist, coach, or mentor. These professionals can provide guidance, tools, and techniques tailored to your specific needs.

Remember that enhancing self-awareness is a continuous practice that requires patience and self-compassion. Celebrate your progress and be gentle with yourself throughout your journey.

Final Thoughts

Why exactly should we be self-aware? What is the magic behind this deeply spiritual practice? No matter what techniques you use, self-awareness is the key to success in interacting with people. Making the effort every day to increase self-awareness will boost performance and satisfaction and improve your life. Author Ralph Ellison asserted in his book *Invisible Man*, "When I discover who I am, I'll be free."

If the self-development journey is 1,000 steps long, the first step must involve becoming one with yourself, the labor of which is self-discovery. It might bring you face-to-face with the parts of yourself you're not so proud of. But you can only win the battle against yourself when you become self-aware.

Chapter Eight

Know Your Strengths

Let me ask you: what are your strengths?

You may find this difficult to answer on the spot. However, this is a common question in job interviews, evaluations, or when decisions are being made about your suitability for a particular opportunity. Knowing your strengths is vital if you are to present the best possible image of yourself.

Let's explore what this question really means.

We answer this question to understand how your unique set of strengths and weaknesses have an impact on you and your goals.

Answering this question can be challenging. It requires a level of self-awareness and self-reflection to understand your personal strengths. For example, if you are applying to graduate school, you will want to focus on your strengths related to study skills. If you are pursuing a sales job, your social skills and ability to connect with people become paramount.

What Exactly Are Strengths?

Strengths are tasks or actions you can perform well. These include knowledge, proficiencies, skills, and talents. People use their traits and abilities to complete work, relate with others, and achieve goals.

The key to succeeding in various situations, personal or professional, is to identify your strengths and ensure they fit the situation or task you are undertaking. Ruch et al. (2014) demonstrated that various types of strengths each have their own significance. The study suggests that these strengths can be categorized into five main types:

1. *Interpersonal Strengths*

These include qualities, such as leadership, teamwork, kindness, forgiveness, and fairness, which enable you to connect with others effectively and foster positive relationships.

2. *Intellectual Strengths*

This category includes traits such as a love of learning, creativity, curiosity, and open-mindedness, all of which drive your intellectual growth and encourage a thirst for knowledge.

3. *Emotional Strengths*

Enthusiasm, hope, and bravery fall under this category. Emotional strengths fuel your optimism, resilience, and courage, empowering you to overcome challenges and embrace life's opportunities.

4. *Strengths of Restraint*

Prudence, self-regulation, and honesty are examples of strengths that help you maintain self-control, make sound decisions, and act with integrity.

5. *Theological Strengths*

Faith, gratitude, and appreciation of beauty fall under this category. These strengths provide you with a sense of purpose, gratitude, and a deep appreciation for the world around you.

Strengths are more than just the activities or skills we are good at. They are the skills and attributes that give us energy and make us feel good, and we achieve great things when we use them. However, each person is unique, and this pattern is not always the case. When you use your strengths, you are energized and motivated. Using your strengths does not just entail doing something you *can* do—it means doing something you *love* doing.

As I work with clients, I help them realize that their strengths represent powerful opportunities to help them grow and feel optimistic about their future. Strengths help them build confidence and self- esteem, making their journey into employment less daunting and difficult. When they realize their strengths, they understand their own uniqueness and motivations and what they are good at. These personal insights can shape their personal and career success by helping them be their most authentic selves.

Now, let's talk about what may de-energize you: weaknesses.

Rather than using the word "weakness," I have found that not focusing on a client's particular weakness leads them to greater self-awareness. Having a weakness does not imply a complete absence of a particular strength. Rather, it means that you may have a lesser degree of that strength or have a potential strength that is not as developed as others.

For example, kindness may be one of my strengths, but I might struggle with teamwork. Some people might possess more intellectual strengths but have fewer theological strengths. Hence, their weaknesses might revolve around faith and gratitude.

Remember, we all have our strengths and weaknesses, and that is perfectly okay. The goal is to understand our strengths so we can harness them effectively and understand our weaknesses so we can work on improving them.

Why Is Knowing Our Strengths Important?

What are your distinctive strengths? Knowing the areas in which you can add the most value through the application of your education, skills, knowledge, and experience can help you focus on the opportunities, roles, and career paths in which you are most likely to succeed and therefore find the greatest sense of accomplishment and contribution. Beyond helping us achieve our goals and reach the pinnacle of success, our strengths contribute to our overall life satisfaction and well-being. Knowing and using your strengths increases your self-belief, builds happiness, and provides positive energy.

Ruch et al. (2014) affirmed that strengths such as gratitude, hope, and love are strongly linked to life satisfaction. Thus, it is necessary to identify our strengths and weaknesses and create a plan to transform our weaknesses into strengths.

Once you know your strengths, it is important to calibrate them just right so that you neither underuse nor overuse them in a given situation. Here's how you can identify your strengths and weaknesses and embark on a path of self-improvement:

Carve Out Dedicated "Self" Time and Unleash the Power of Self-Discovery

To grasp the essence of your being, you must dedicate undisturbed time to self-reflection. Set aside a generous 20–30 minutes of uninterrupted focus once a week. This sacred time will provide you with the opportunity to dive deeply into your innermost self and unleash the hidden truths of your strengths and weaknesses. Prepare yourself for an exhilarating experience of self-discovery through the art of targeted questioning. Begin by asking yourself these probing questions: What are my undeniable strengths and weaknesses? How do I identify and validate them? How do these strengths and weaknesses manifest in my daily life? Are there other complementary strengths or weaknesses that contribute to my behavior?

Allow your answers to guide you through this enchanting exploration. Feel free to seek inspiration from online lists of common strengths and weaknesses to get yourself started.

Self-reflection and self-improvement are ongoing processes, so make it a habit to assess your strengths and weaknesses regularly. Set aside time every few months to reflect on your growth, reassess your strengths, and identify areas for improvement. This practice will help you stay on track and ensure that you continue to evolve and unlock your full potential.

Reflect for a Minute

Another avenue through which to unlock the secrets of your strengths and weaknesses lies within your experiences. Take a moment to recollect instances that have led to exceptional outcomes (for strengths) or less-than-desirable results (for weaknesses). It may be a triumph in supporting a friend or a team endeavor that fell short of your expectations.

Now turn to the spiritual compass of introspection, and ask yourself the following: Which skills or strengths contributed to my success? What other factors played a role in the outcome? Can I identify any hidden elements that influenced my actions or decisions? Embrace the wisdom that emerges from these reflections.

Allow them to shape your understanding of yourself because these experiences are a gateway to your hidden potential.

Seek the Perspective of Others

Once you have gained some insights into your strengths and weaknesses, consider seeking the guidance of a friend who knows you well. Their unique perspective can provide you with a fresh lens through which to view yourself. No one achieves greatness alone. Surround yourself with a supportive network of individuals who believe in your potential and encourage your growth. Collaborate with like-minded individuals who complement your strengths and can help you overcome your weaknesses. Build relationships with mentors who can provide guidance and advice based on their experiences. A strong support network will provide valuable insights and growth opportunities. However, remember that their opinions are subjective, and it is important to reflect on the insights of others before internalizing them.

Only when you master the secret to self-awareness will you pave the way for personal growth and professional success. Unearth your strengths and weaknesses and let them become beacons of light guiding you toward an extraordinary future.

Embrace the Uniqueness of You

Understanding your strengths is akin to unlocking the secret to your brilliance. These are the areas in which you effortlessly shine and excel—the realms where your unique talents make an indelible impact. Embrace your strengths and allow them to become the foundation on which you build your path to success.

Conversely, your weaknesses need not hold you back—they are merely opportunities for growth and self-improvement. Take a proactive approach to addressing your weaknesses. Seek learning opportunities, attend conferences or workshops, and continuously strive to refine your skills. Remember that even the most minor weaknesses can be transformed into essential business skills through practice and dedication.

Seek Learning and Development Opportunities

To enhance your strengths and address your weaknesses further, actively seek out learning and development opportunities. Attend workshops, seminars, or training programs that focus on your areas of interest and expertise. Engage in continuous learning through books, podcasts, online courses, or mentorship programs. When you invest in your growth, you expand your knowledge and skills, making yourself even more valuable.

Leverage Your Strengths

Once you have a solid grasp of your strengths, find ways to leverage them in your personal and professional endeavors. Seek opportunities that align with your strengths and allow you to showcase them. Whether this means taking on projects that highlight your unique skills or pursuing a career path that capitalizes on your personal attributes, embracing and utilizing your strengths will increase your chances of success and fulfillment.

Take Your Strengths to New Heights With the Four Cs

Let's talk about tapping into your potential and skyrocketing your life to extraordinary heights.

Do you ever feel like your true talents are lying dormant, waiting to be discovered?

Well, I've got some eye-opening insights for you.

We often get caught up in fixing our shortcomings instead of nurturing our natural gifts. It is time to break free from staying too long in the *fix-your-weaknesses* mindset that has been holding you back.

And guess what? Our greatest opportunity for growth and improvement lies in uncovering and developing our strengths. It's time to recognize what makes us special and let our brilliance shine!

Research has shown that when we actively focus on and cultivate our strengths, the results are mind-blowing. We experience greater happiness, reduced stress, a surge of energy, boosted confidence, and accelerated personal growth. Your biggest opportunity for improvement and growth is by improving your strengths as opposed to your weaknesses. Try this little exercise below to sharpen your strengths.

Write out your favorite three strengths. Then, for each strength, ask yourself:

- What opportunities are out there for me?

- How could I use this strength more?

- What is underneath this strength and how could I turn this strength into an opportunity?

- What ideas could I really enjoy doing that I have been putting off?

- Where could I use this strength to make a difference in my life, career, and relationships?

- Where could I really shine if I just let myself?

Then brainstorm and write below a quick three-to-five bullet- point action plan of what you could do to boost your strengths!

Finally, once done, circle *one* action from each strength that you will consider doing this week. Who wouldn't want a piece of that action?

So, let's dive into the game-changing four Cs that will help you unlock your strengths and soar to new heights:

1. First Up, Curiosity.

It is time to be a detective of your own potential. Explore what makes your heart race and your soul come alive. Discover the activities, projects, and passions that ignite your inner fire. Explore your available resources and uncover the path to developing your unique talents. Embrace your curiosity, and let it guide you to greatness!

2. *Next, Let Your Creativity Run Wild*

Break free from the ordinary and dare to think outside the box. Every single day, challenge yourself to find new ways to leverage your strengths for your own benefit. Don't overanalyze or overwhelm yourself—just take things one step at a time.

For example, if you're a master of organization at work but struggle at home, why not sprinkle some of that organizational magic into your personal life? Let your creativity flow and watch the magic unfold!

3. *Now, Confidence Is Your Secret Weapon*

Believe in yourself with unwavering conviction. Half the battle of overcoming an obstacle is simply believing in your ability to conquer it. Remember that the biggest hurdle you'll face is often the battle in your own mind. Sure, there may be tough days where self- doubt creeps in, but you always have the ability to realign and get back on track. Let your confidence be the fuel that propels you forward, igniting your path to greatness!

4. *Lastly, Find the Power in Creating a Plan*

Create a road map that is laser-focused on developing your greatest strengths. Set tangible goals that resonate with your passions and aspirations. Jot them down and assign each one a target date. Be realistic and remember to review your goals frequently to stay on track. Make your goals impossible to ignore by posting them where you will see them all day—on your refrigerator, the bathroom mirror, or your computer screen.

Let these visual reminders fuel your motivation and drive you toward rapid goal-crushing success. And if you stumble while crafting your plan, reflect on how your core strengths can come to the rescue in potentially stressful situations.

You've got this!

Final Thoughts

Now, remember this: you may not be able to be everything, but you certainly can be the best version of yourself—the real you. As you progress on your journey of self-improvement, take time to celebrate your successes, both big and small. Acknowledge your achievements and milestones along the way to not only boost your confidence but also reinforce your commitment to your personal growth. Remind yourself of how far you have come and motivate yourself to keep pushing forward.

Embrace your authenticity, and let your strengths illuminate the world. It is time to unleash your superpowers and create an extraordinary life.

So, are you ready to embark on this exhilarating journey of self-discovery and growth? Buckle up, my friend, because your extraordinary adventure awaits!

Chapter Nine

New Habits

Habits.

We are all creatures of habit. I know I am. I tend to wake up at the same time each day: I transfer to my wheelchair, take care of my hygiene, have my morning coffee, and turn on my computer. What we think, feel, and do each day is directed by our subconscious far more often than we realize. Through repetition, our brain creates shortcuts, which are automatic responses developed over time due to associated learning. This is what allows us to move through many activities of daily life without having to really think about them. As far as the brain is concerned, the more tasks you can complete without wasting time thinking about them, the better.

What exactly is a habit? Our habits shape who we are. They are our tendency to do something, whether good or bad. A good routine will help you reach your goals, develop your life personally and professionally, and help you feel fulfilled. Bad habits do the opposite. Both good and bad habits are often triggered by something specific. For instance, walking past a bakery and smelling pastries can trigger your craving for a cookie, or a stressful meeting at work triggers you to bite your nails.

Have you ever wondered how long it takes to form a new habit? Contrary to popular belief, there is no magic number of days.

Habits do not just magically appear after a specific number of repetitions. They develop gradually over time in a nonlinear fashion.

Initially, conscious repetition of behavior leads to quick progress in automating that behavior. Your brain refines the process as you practice more, and the behavior becomes second nature. It is very much like a recipe for preparing a dish in the kitchen. Over time, you will find it easier to develop the successful daily habits you want to incorporate into your routine.

Interestingly, once a habit takes hold, it is no longer driven by internal motivations and goals. It becomes an automatic response to environmental cues. With knowledge and willpower, we can shape our environments and consciously develop desired habits that align with our aspirations.

So, why is it so effortless to fall into the trap of bad habits yet incredibly challenging to cultivate good ones?

Forming new habits is hard, and breaking unhealthy habits is even harder. Though it is a conundrum we have all faced, building positive daily habits is one of the few things that have the potential to transform your life. Unfortunately, the sad truth is that a year from now, you will likely find yourself stuck in the same old habits instead of embracing a better version of yourself. A successful habit formation approach needs to consider all these things. What will work for a person with a particular living situation and set of likes and dislikes will not work for someone else who differs substantively in these areas. Often, the things immediately rewarding in our environment are different from those that meet our long-term goals. We have yet to manage to organize the environment in a way that allows us to form good habits easily. Even with sincere efforts and occasional bursts of motivation, sustaining good habits beyond a few days can seem overwhelming. Whether it is exercise, meditation, journaling, or cooking healthy meals, they start off as promising but quickly become burdensome. In contrast, unwanted habits tend to cling to us like stubborn weeds.

Breaking free from this cycle is challenging for two reasons: we attempt to change the wrong thing and go about it in the wrong way. Shifting our focus to the first layer of behavior change; we can envision it as the outermost layer of an onion. This layer revolves around changing our outcomes, the tangible results we desire— shedding pounds, publishing a book, or winning a championship. Most of our goals fall into this category.

The second layer digs deeper into it because it focuses on changing the processes that lie behind forming the habits and systems we adopt— establishing a workout routine, organizing our workspace for optimal productivity, and finding a space to meditate. Many of the habits we build belong here.

But at the core lies the third and most profound layer: changing our identity. This layer transforms our beliefs, self-perceptions, and judgments about ourselves and others. When we align our behaviors and thoughts with our values, it helps us focus on what we determine to be right or wrong, good or bad. A few examples of core values include family, personal growth, gratitude, assertiveness, dependability, integrity, and courage. Your values keep you on track and never let you stray too far (or at all) from who you are. When you make decisions through the lens of your values, those decisions allow you to discover all of your choices so that you can make the best decisions based on all your options.

Now, here's where it gets interesting.

When it comes to building lasting habits and achieving consistent improvement, it is essential to understand the value of different levels in the habit-building process. Instead of focusing solely on the desired outcomes, it is more powerful to cultivate identity-based habits that align with the person we aspire to become. Let me illustrate this with a different example.

Consider two individuals who are offered a dessert. The first person declines, saying, "No thanks. I'm trying to lose weight." Although this response seems reasonable, deep down, they still identify themselves as someone struggling with their weight. They hope their behavior will change while holding onto the same beliefs. In contrast, the second person declines by stating, "No thanks. I'm not someone who indulges in desserts." This seemingly insignificant response signifies a shift in identity. They no longer view themselves as someone who regularly consumes desserts. Their identity has changed, and they align their behavior accordingly. Many people fail to consider identity change when they embark on self-improvement journeys. They set goals and determine actions without reflecting on the underlying beliefs that drive their behavior.

However, behavior incongruent with our self-perception cannot be sustained.

Let us broaden our perspective further. Just as a system of beliefs underpins the functioning of different political systems, our personal habits are also shaped by a set of beliefs and assumptions— the identity behind them. For example, if your identity revolves around being a spender rather than a saver, you may crave financial abundance but find yourself perpetually drawn toward spending instead of saving. Similarly, if you prioritize comfort over achievement, even if you desire optimal health, you will find solace in relaxation rather than pushing yourself to exercise. Changing our habits becomes challenging when we fail to address the underlying beliefs that guided our past behaviors. It is not enough to have new goals and plans; we must genuinely transform who we are at our core.

The ultimate level of intrinsic motivation occurs when a habit seamlessly integrates into our identity. Saying, "I'm the type of person who desires this," is one thing, but declaring, "I'm the type of person who embodies this," takes it to a different level. The more pride we derive from a specific aspect of our identity, the more inclined we are to maintain the habits associated with it. If we take pride in our knowledge as a reader, we will develop various rituals to read consistently and expand our literary horizons. If we are proud of our discipline as a runner, we will ensure we never skip a scheduled run. If we identify ourselves as dedicated musicians, we will spend hours perfecting our musical skills. Pride becomes intertwined with our habits, and thus we fight to preserve them. In truth, genuine behavior change equates to identity change. Although motivation can initiate a habit, it is the integration into our identity that ensures its longevity. Anyone can convince themselves to engage in certain actions temporarily, but without a shift in belief, sustaining long-term changes becomes an uphill battle. Progress remains temporary until it solidifies and becomes part of your identity.

Remember, the goal is not merely to read a book; it is to become a reader. It is not just about completing a marathon; it is about embodying the identity of a runner. Learning an instrument is not an endpoint but a journey to becoming a musician. Your behavior reflects your identity. What you do mirrors the type of person you believe yourself to be, whether consciously or unconsciously. Doing the right thing becomes effortless because your behavior harmonizes with your identity. At this point, it is no longer about changing habits but rather about embodying the person you already perceive yourself to be.

However, there is a catch. Identity changes, like all aspects of habit formation, have a dual nature. When it works in your favor, it becomes a powerful catalyst for self-improvement. However, when it works against you, it can act as a curse. Once you adopt an identity, it can hinder your ability to change. Many individuals adhere blindly to the norms tied to their identity, creating resistance to certain actions because "that's not who I am." The deeper the connection between a thought or action and our identity, the more challenging it becomes to modify it. The beliefs of our culture or our self-perception can be comfortable to adopt, even if they hinder progress. The greatest hurdle to positive change lies in identity conflict, regardless of whether it is at an individual, team, or societal level. Even though good habits make logical sense, we struggle to put them into action if they clash with our identity.

On any given day, you may encounter challenges with your habits, such as business, fatigue, or a myriad of other reasons. Yet, in the grand scheme of things, the primary reason for failure to stick with habits is the obstruction caused by your self-image. That is precisely why you should not become overly attached to a single version of your identity. Progress necessitates unlearning and embracing the flexibility of growth. Many of us assume those hyper-achievers who effortlessly fit in their workouts, maintain healthy eating habits, excel in their jobs, and pick up their children on time possess an extraordinary level of self-control. However, scientific findings suggest a different answer: what we often mistake for sheer willpower is, in fact, a testimony to habit. Individuals with good habits seldom need to resist the temptation to laze on the couch, indulge in greasy takeout foods, procrastinate on projects, or watch one more viral video before rushing out the door. They have harnessed the power of autopilot, which eliminates the allure of temptation.

We all understand the mechanics of good habits, right? Well, guess what? The same principles apply when it comes to bidding farewell to those pesky habits that no longer serve you. Bad habits, from picking at your nails to smoking, may feel good at the time, but in the long term, they have negative physical, emotional, and psychological consequences that can interrupt your life and stop you from accomplishing your goals. We all know what bad habits are, but not everyone refers to them as that. Here are other ways you may engage in bad habits:

Smoking—research shows that even in small quantities, smoking is bad for you. However, the benefits of quitting begin just 20 minutes after your last cigarette (Jha, 2020).

Not exercising—this is a bad habit that is not as obviously bad for you as smoking. But sometimes bad habits can simply be inaction. Exercising is important for your health and mental state (Mandolesi et al., 2018). It might be helpful to start by exercising in small chunks, such as 15 minutes in the morning and 15 minutes after work, to get a good half hour of exercise a day.

Too much screen time before bed—one way to get more sleep is to break the common bad habit of looking at a screen right before you go to bed. Some research has shown that light from electronics such as TVs, tablets, and smartphones can mess with the hormones that help us sleep (Gringras et al., 2015). Instead, it may help to do mindfulness meditations or engage in activities such as reading before bed.

Overspending—one of the most common ways to deal with stress is to engage in buying things we do not necessarily need. This can easily lead to people developing debt if unchecked, so it may help to make a budget or plan to check your accounts often to avoid this.

Procrastination—I know I am guilty of this, but we often do not give ourselves enough time to do what we have planned. Usually, people procrastinate because they are either perfectionists or lazy.

Either way, it may help to try and make a schedule (and stick to it) to get things done in time.

Negative self-talk—too often, people cannot say anything nice about themselves. We are often taught to be our own worst critics, which can sometimes become overwhelming and may lead to low self-esteem. This is why it is good to engage in positive self-talk; encouraging yourself may help you to look on the brighter side of situations and ultimately feel better. Habits can be hard to break once they become deeply wired in our brains after many repetitions, but there are ways to change them.

The Power of Routines and How to Build Healthy Habits

Understanding the mechanics of habit formation is a game- changer. Educate yourself about the science behind habits, and you will gain a significant advantage in creating and maintaining healthy routines. When you read and absorb knowledge, you are already taking a proactive step toward making positive change. We tend to overlook the importance of daily habits in managing ourselves and our lives. But it is often small changes to daily routines that enable people to make significant changes in their lives and careers.

For most people, the word *routine* conjures up images of a boring, repetitive life, with every moment controlled and managed— no room for spontaneity. This may have been especially true during the COVID-19 pandemic, when routines may have felt boring and restrictive.

But trust me, it is anything but! As a coach, I know that establishing routines can be a powerful tool. To be able to live to the fullest in this complex reality, our brains have developed a cognitive system that helps organize all the information we receive on a minute-by-minute basis. We categorize objects, colors, sounds, smells, or movements to simplify and organize our reality. We organize our behaviors in a similar way. Sometimes it happens consciously, such as when we meticulously organize our mornings to set us up for a good mood that will last throughout the day.

But sometimes, we create rituals unconsciously. For example, some people repeat the same movements every time they begin eating, whereas others prefer to drink their coffee from the same mug while sitting in the same chair every morning. These small or big rituals play a crucial role in our lives: not only do they provide us with predictability, security, and control, but they help us structure our time and behavior to deal with the chaos around us.

Routines do more than just keeping us in check. They supercharge our cognitive function, boost our overall health, and serve as meaningful activities that bring joy and fulfillment. They are the secret ingredient that adds spontaneity, fun, and countless social opportunities to our lives. *Sounds amazing, right?*

Well, here's the best part: building your own routine is as easy as one, two, and three!

Step one: Identify the task. Take a moment to reflect on what you truly desire. Maybe you crave that precious "me time" for at least an hour each day.

Step two: Identify the time or trigger. Discover the perfect moment to infuse your routine with energy. Is it the tranquil morning hours or the rejuvenating midafternoon?

Step three: Identify the subtasks. Break down your routine into manageable steps. Find a serene sanctuary, close the door to distractions, silence your phone, and give yourself the gift of uninterrupted bliss for 45 minutes to an hour.

There is no secret one-size-fits-all solution and no magic button. Welcome the adventure of exploring different methods and discovering what works best for you. Many find that combining various routines and productivity methods creates a powerful system tailored to their unique needs. With a well-crafted routine in place, you will not have to reinvent the wheel every time you face a challenge. Adapt, modify, and evolve your routine as you see fit, ensuring it aligns with your ever-changing aspirations.

Be prepared to view your daily routines as mighty tools that drive you toward success. One of my favorite quotes is from John C. Maxwell, a best-selling author and leadership coach, who stated, "You'll never change your life until you change something you do daily. The secret of your success is found in your daily routine."

This hits home with many of my clients because it helps them develop routines that remove unnecessary decision-making and allows them to focus on what they most want and need to accomplish their goals. Let these words resonate within you as you develop routines that eliminate unnecessary decision-making and allow you to focus on what truly matters—the fulfillment of your dreams and the accomplishment of your goals.

The way we perceive a habit plays a significant role in its success. If a habit seems daunting, it becomes more challenging to sustain. Instead, break it down into manageable steps and start small. Begin with actions that are so easy that you cannot say no. For example, if you want to jog five times a week, start by putting on your workout attire. The next day, step outside your door. Gradually increase the intensity and duration of your exercise routine as your confidence grows. Remember, every journey begins with a single step. Focus on establishing the habit itself before fine-tuning and optimizing it. Make it a priority to show up consistently. For instance, if you want to develop a habit of writing every day, start by committing to writing for just 10 minutes a day. Make it a non- negotiable part of your routine. Once you have ingrained the habit of writing consistently, you can gradually increase the duration and improve the quality of your writing.

Although change is never easy, a good start to breaking bad habits can be to increase your awareness. It is easy to get stuck on how our bad habits make us feel, but it may be more helpful to try to make a change instead. Monitoring your progress is a powerful way to stay motivated and hold yourself accountable. Use a habit tracker or journal to record your daily activities and track your consistency. Reflecting on your progress will help you identify patterns, make adjustments, stay on track toward your goals, and learn from any setbacks.

In addition, surround yourself with a supportive community or find an accountability partner who shares your commitment to building habits. Having someone to share your journey with, exchange ideas, and provide encouragement can significantly enhance your chances of success. Share your goals and progress with them, and together you can celebrate milestones and navigate challenges.

Building habits takes time and effort. There will be days when motivation wanes, or obstacles arise. During those moments, remind yourself of your deeper reasons for wanting to establish the habit. Revisit your goals, visualize the long-term benefits, and find ways to reignite your determination. Remember that setbacks are part of the process, and the most important thing is to keep going. If you stumble or miss a day, do not let it derail you completely. Failure is an opportunity for growth and self-reflection. Analyze what led to the lapse, identify any triggers or obstacles, and brainstorm strategies to overcome them in the future. Embrace failure as a chance to learn, adjust, and become more resilient on your habit-building journey.

Celebrate milestones too! Recognize and celebrate your progress along the way. Set smaller milestones within your larger habit-building goal and reward yourself when you achieve them. The rewards can be as simple as treating yourself to a favorite activity or indulging in something you enjoy. Celebrating milestones boosts your motivation and reinforces the positive association with the habit you are building.

Final Thoughts

I invite you to harness the power of habits and routines to solidify the lessons we have learned together. Habits are a mirror of our thoughts, actions, and, ultimately, our destiny. They possess the remarkable ability to shape our character, define our achievements, and determine our level of fulfillment. Although habits can be both constructive and insidious, the key lies in recognizing their power and consciously leveraging it. When we integrate desired behaviors into our identity, we can create lasting change. Shifting our focus from mere outcomes to identity-based habits allows us to embody the person we aspire to be, paving the way for consistent growth and transformation.

Breaking free from unwanted habits requires understanding the underlying beliefs that drive them. It demands unlearning and embracing the flexibility of growth. When we address our self-image and challenge identity conflicts, we can overcome the resistance to change and forge a path toward positive transformation. Building healthy habits is a gradual process that requires patience, perseverance, and self-awareness. We can start small, focusing on triggers and monitoring our progress. We can then lay a solid foundation for lasting change.

You may not be successful all the time, but that does not mean you are not making meaningful steps in the right direction. It is more important to be persistent and kind to yourself on your journey. Ultimately, habits are not just routines but the building blocks of our lives. With conscious intention and a commitment to personal growth, we can shape our habits and, in turn, our destiny.

Chapter Ten

Communication

"Speak clearly, if you speak at all; carve every word before you let it fall."

— *Oliver Wendell Holmes, Sr.*

On a daily basis, we communicate to and with others. Whether it's the watercooler chitchat you have with your coworkers at work, the level of attention you give your spouse when they are talking to you, or the look or stare you give your pet, it all means something. We live in a world where communication can be a powerful tool that uplifts your personal and professional relationships.

When you think of the word "communication," what do you think of? Many people will think of the spoken word. People who are hard of hearing, however, might think of sign language. People who are visually impaired might think of Braille as well as sounds. I want to invite you into a world where your words have the power to inspire, motivate, and create a lasting impact.

The English dictionary defines communication as "the imparting or interchange of thoughts, opinions, or information by speech, writing, or signs." Many of us love connecting with other people because it makes us happy, and good communication is the key to positive social interaction.

But let's be honest, sometimes it feels like we're speaking different languages, even when using the same words. Misunderstandings, frustrations, and conflicts can arise, leaving us longing for a better way to connect. Communication is one of the most important aspects of life and touches on all areas, including your career, personal life, and even interactions with strangers.

It is important to take a positive approach to communication and remember that people are hugely influenced by what you say and how you say it. The best communicators know that to get the best out of others—you need to stimulate and engage with them. If you frame things in a positive way and be mindful of what you communicate (e.g., avoid gossip and criticisms), the odds are you will feel better and attract interested and interesting people. You will also have a positive mindset and spot more opportunities. The ability to communicate is not an innate skill; it is something we can and should develop as we progress through life. Unfortunately, most do not take the time to focus on how well they communicate and leave this important element to chance. Those who do take the time to develop this key skill will likely find that they are pleasantly surprised by the results. Successful communication is a two-way process, sending as well as receiving. You must first present your ideas in a form others can understand and then listen to others to understand how your message is being received. This mutual understanding is necessary if the purpose of communication is to be achieved.

This is where effective communication comes in. It's not all about exchanging words; it's about making the most of every situation. To understand how to improve your communication skills, you must first know what it means to communicate effectively.

Awareness of effective communication is becoming increasingly important. We deal with sending and receiving telephone, email, blog, forum, text, and face-to-face messages every day.

When you communicate effectively, you build rapport, develop relationships, and feel comfortable and confident in your interactions. You become a master at getting others to open up, sharing their feelings and thoughts. You navigate difficult conversations with grace and respond thoughtfully. The pressure eases, and you feel a weight lifted off your shoulders.

Effective communication skills reduce misunderstandings and build empathy and understanding between people, especially in relationships. Communication is like cooking a pot of authentic Louisiana gumbo. It's an art that requires practice and finesse and the right flavors and ingredients, but when mastered, oh boy, watch out! *Laissez les bon temps rouler!*

Here are some practical tips and strategies to help you enhance your communication skills:

1. *Practice Active Listening*

Let's tune our ears to the sweet melodies of active listening. Instead of being preoccupied with what to say next or passing judgment, be fully present and engaged in the conversation. Give your communication partner the invaluable gift of feeling heard and valued. Trust me, when you lend your ears and your heart, collaboration and cooperation become second nature. Engage fully in conversations by giving your undivided attention. Listen attentively, maintain eye contact, and avoid interrupting. Show genuine interest in what the other person is saying and ask clarifying questions to ensure understanding.

Imagine for a moment that you're in a conversation with someone you barely know or someone close to you, like your spouse, children, or boss. Now brace yourself for the unexpected. As you apply the skills I'm about to share, you'll be astounded by the profound impact they have on your interactions. Allow me to paint you a picture.

The secret to a remarkable conversation lies in active listening, an art that involves withholding our own ideas and wholeheartedly embracing the thoughts and concerns of the other person. Remember, if someone is worth speaking to, they are certainly worth listening to. To truly engage in active listening, start by displaying genuine interest through eye contact and leaning slightly forward, creating a safe and welcoming space. Begin the conversation with a simple inquiry like, "How are you doing?" or "How's it going?" This opens the door for the other person to share their concerns and ideas.

Encourage them to delve deeper by saying something like, "Tell me more about your job, classes, or retirement."

Alternatively, echo their words, reflecting on what they just said. This reassures them that you are genuinely interested and encourages them to continue sharing.

2. *Be Mindful of Nonverbal Cues*

Good communication enhances relationships. When you actively listen and offer quality feedback, you make others feel heard and understood. This nurtures mutual respect and strengthens the bonds between individuals. Let's acknowledge that unhealthy communication often stems from negative thoughts and challenging emotions. Remember that words are merely the echoes of those thoughts and feelings. To cultivate healthier communication, start by recognizing and understanding your own emotions; immerse yourself in them and then express them in a way that develops connection and understanding. Communication is not just about words; it also involves nonverbal cues such as facial expressions, body language, and tone of voice. Pay attention to your own nonverbal signals and be aware of those of others. Use open and welcoming body language to create a positive and inclusive atmosphere.

3. Use Clear and Concise Language

Clarity is key. When conveying your message, be aware of the lens through which you interpret information. Sometimes it's beneficial to put on your paraphrasing hat: summarize what you've understood in your own words, ensuring that you've grasped the essence of the other person's words. This will not only help you clarify any potential misunderstandings but also show that you genuinely care about their perspective. Avoid jargon, complex terms, or ambiguous phrases that might confuse others. Strive for clarity and simplicity in your communication. Use concrete examples and specific details to convey your message effectively. Clear communication sets the stage for success. When you concisely deliver expectations and objectives, you empower your team members to understand their roles and responsibilities. This clarity eliminates confusion and conflict, fostering a more productive and harmonious work environment.

4. Adapt Your Communication Style and Be Aware of Cultural Differences

Recognize that different people have different communication preferences. Adjust your approach based on whom you are interacting with. Some people may prefer a direct and assertive communication style, while others may respond better to a more diplomatic and empathetic approach. In a diverse world; it's also important to be mindful of cultural nuances in communication. Different cultures have unique communication styles and norms. Educate yourself about cultural differences and adapt your communication accordingly to promote understanding and avoid misunderstanding.

5. Practice Empathy

Put yourself in the other person's shoes and try to understand their perspective. Show empathy by acknowledging their feelings and validating their experiences. This helps build trust and foster a positive connection. According to Fortin et al. (2019), the name, understand, respect, and support (NURS) approach is a means to do that.

Begin by naming the emotion, acknowledging the other person's experience with statements like, "So that makes you feel sad, depressed, angry, upset, afraid, relieved, or happy."

Next, demonstrate your understanding with phrases such as, "I can understand how you would feel that way" or "I see how you feel."

Validate their emotions by emphasizing that anyone would feel the same in their situation. Respect their emotional journey by acknowledging their struggles with statements like, "This has been a difficult time for you," or "You've been through a lot." Offer praise for their resilience and efforts, acknowledging their hard work or courage.

6. *Use Positive Language*

Embrace the power of positivity. When addressing needs and concerns, it's essential to maintain a respectful tone. Yes, it's okay to feel angry or frustrated, but let's not forget the importance of highlighting the positive aspects of what we desire. Use positive and encouraging language to inspire and motivate others. Instead of focusing on what went wrong, highlight strengths and solutions. When you have addressed needs and concerns, state the positive aspects of what you require and how it will benefit the individual. For instance, "If we manage to complete this report by late Wednesday evening, we can avoid staying overnight and can be home all day Thursday to spend time with our families." Positive language creates a supportive environment and encourages collaboration.

7. *Practice Assertiveness*

Assertiveness involves expressing your thoughts, opinions, and needs in a respectful and confident manner. Find a balance between being too passive and too aggressive. Assertive communication promotes mutual understanding and helps you advocate for yourself while considering the needs of others.

As you continue the conversation using supportive comments, be attentive to cues that hint at underlying emotions. Guide their focus toward these emotions by saying, "Tell me more about the pain of losing your friend," or "Share your feelings about being denied access to the gym."

Here's a pro tip: people often touch upon emotional topics briefly before diverting to another subject, testing the waters to see if you genuinely want to delve into their emotional world. Pay close attention and steer them back to these important emotional issues.

As you navigate the tension-laden territory and gain a deeper understanding of their situation, it's time to unearth the emotions themselves. Probe gently when asking questions and aim to comprehend the nuances of their emotional landscape. For instance, encourage a person to elaborate on being depressed, angry, upset, or relieved.

However, remember that understanding emotions may not always come easily. Some individuals may resist expressing their emotions, stating, "I don't know, I guess I feel nothing. My family never talked about feelings." In such cases, explore further by offering your own perspective, saying something like, "If I were in your shoes, I might feel upset." Be mindful of their comfort level and choose milder terms like "upset" or "distressed" instead of potentially overwhelming words like "angry" or "depressed."

If the emotions remain elusive despite your efforts, that's perfectly fine. Release the pressure and let it go. Don't force someone into discomfort. By now, you likely have uncovered emotions such as sadness, anger, happiness, or depression.

8. *Seek and Practice Active Feedback*

Actively encourage feedback from others to understand how your communication is perceived. Be open to constructive criticism and make adjustments accordingly. This helps you identify areas for improvement and refine your communication skills. Provide feedback to others in a constructive and specific manner. Focus on the behavior or situation rather than personal attacks. Offer suggestions for improvement and recognize their strengths. This helps foster a culture of continuous improvement and growth. Positive feedback is not only a boost for the person receiving it, but it also works as a great motivator and will help encourage the receiver to continue their good work. Complimenting people also helps develop empathy and positive feelings and cultivates positive relationships that make future communication much easier. The benefits of giving positive feedback are obvious, but people can still be reluctant to offer it.

Part of the reason people are hesitant to give positive feedback is that it can feel quite awkward complimenting someone, and we often worry about wording feedback incorrectly and perhaps sounding stupid. It's important to realize, though, that even awkwardly presented feedback is better than no feedback at all.

Remember that effective communication is a skill to be developed and refined with practice. Start implementing these strategies in your daily interactions, and over time you will see their positive impact on your relationships and overall communication effectiveness.

Remember to sprinkle these NURS statements throughout the conversation sparingly and genuinely. For instance, you might start by saying, "That's upsetting, and I can certainly understand." After listening for another brief period, respond with "You've had a tough time," or "Good for you for talking about it." Allow these statements to flow naturally, enriching your connection with the other person.

Keep in mind that you're not expected to become a therapist or solve everybody's problems. It's natural to worry about opening a can of worms when you hear about someone's challenging circumstances such as a divorce, job loss, or serious illness. However, remember that simply lending an empathetic ear and practicing NURS can provide tremendous relief and comfort. Often, people in dire situations crave understanding, respect, and support more than anything else. The act of listening with empathy has an astonishing healing effect.

Using the DISC Assessment to Break Down Communication Walls

As discussed throughout this chapter, communication is the foundation of building relationships. Whether you are at work, at home, or simply on the street, you will alienate people and convey messages in the wrong way if you have poor communication skills. This can lead to conflict and other problems, causing tense situations in places where you should be able to relax, enjoy yourself, and focus on the things that really matter. To improve communication with new clients, I use an assessment tool before embarking on my coaching journey with them. This dominance, influence, steadiness, and conscientiousness (DISC) assessment is a fascinating tool rooted in our behavioral styles. It provides insights into building effective communication skills and nonjudgmental results that help people communicate better as they discover and discuss their behavioral differences. This powerful tool opens the doorway to effective communication, allowing modification of language and behavior, communication patterns, and reactions in various situations. I have found that people respond better to those they like and understand.

The DISC assessment is based on the early work of William Moulton Marston, who is a lawyer, psychologist, and inventor of a component of the lie detector. Drawing on Marston's groundbreaking work, the

DISC assessment offers a simple yet transformative framework for understanding ourselves and others. Each person possesses a unique blend of the examined traits, with varying degrees of strength in each category. It serves as a universal language, deciphering the intricate dance of human behavior and speech. By recognizing the DISC profile of the person with whom we're engaging, we can adapt our communication style to align with their preferences rather than imposing our own.

Moreover, this approach unveils their predictable behaviors and dominant personality traits, all of which profoundly impact personal growth, relationships, career progression, and other aspects of life. Armed with this knowledge, I use the *Taking Flight With DISC* version created by author Merrick Rosenberg (2015) and EO of Take Flight Learning, a training company. Because many people admit they don't remember what the letters stand for weeks later, his version of DISC swapped out the classic letters (i.e., D, I, S, and C) for a more visual and memorable approach, using birds—eagle, parrot, dove, and owl—to symbolize the styles. By linking eagles to the **D**ominant style, parrots to the **I**nfluence style, doves to the **S**teadiness style, and owls to the **C**onscientiousness style, people remember the approach better.

By using this approach, I establish a common language with my clients, providing more seamless and harmonious communication throughout our sessions.

Eagle. When communicating with an "eagle," remember their focus on results and the big picture. They represent the "D" in the DISC model. They exude confidence, directness, and a no-nonsense demeanor. The eagle style is fast-paced and action-oriented. People who embody the eagle know what they want and are driven to achieve their goals quickly. They are outgoing, confident in their abilities, and have no problem telling you what they're thinking. Their self- assurance enables them to take on challenges where they can launch initiatives for bigger and better results. Are you bold, daring, direct, confident, and decisive? If so, you have some of the eagle style within you.

Parrot. Those with this style, which represents the "I" style in the DISC model, recognize their people-centric mindset, driven by their connections with others. They radiate enthusiasm, optimism, trust, and boundless energy. The parrot style is people-oriented and optimistic. Sociable, influential, and motivational, they are always looking on the bright side, because parrots see the best in everyone they meet and can find fun in nearly any situation. Their high energy and creativity are contagious, so if you're not paying attention, you may just get swept up in their latest adventure. Are you optimistic, enthusiastic, motivational, and always have a good story to share? If so, you probably have some parrot style in you.

Dove. When engaging with a "dove," understand their emphasis on cooperation, sincerity, loyalty, and dependability. They represent the "S" style in the DISC model. They possess a calm, deliberate disposition and disdain for being rushed. The dove style is supportive and empathetic. People attuned to the dove style bring harmony wherever they go and create a safe, stable, and predictable environment for themselves and others. They tend to be soft-spoken and enjoy close relationships in tight circles. Doves are always there for you when you need them, whether being a good listener or helping when times get tough. Do you value sincerity, stability, and helpfulness? If so, you probably have some dove in you.

Owl. When communicating with an "owl," bear in mind their detail-oriented nature and preference for stability. They prioritize quality, accuracy, expertise, and competency, representing the "C" style in the DISC model. Independence is cherished, and attention to minutiae is a defining trait, often accompanied by a fear of making mistakes. The owl style is deliberate and precise. People who exhibit owl characteristics value quality and live by the motto, "If you're going to do something, do it right the first time." They are logical, systematic, and conscientious. Naturally deep thinkers, owls are great at complex projects where organization is key to success. As leaders, they make sure processes and systems are clearly defined. If you have ever been impressed by how smoothly something worked, you have been in the presence of an owl. Are you driven by logic, accuracy, and high standards? If so, you probably have some owl style in you.

It's important to note that no one DISC style is superior to another. The framework is devoid of judgment because we all exhibit aspects of each style in our daily lives. However, the DISC assessment helps us identify our predominant style and comfort zone, enabling us to understand our underlying tendencies and preferences.

Equipped with this self-awareness, we can adapt our behaviors to foster more effective interactions and communication with others. Personally, I gravitate toward the parrot style. You may have witnessed someone like me in a tense meeting where voices overlap and tensions run high. Suddenly someone calls for a momentary pause, suggesting, "Can we step back for a minute? I believe there's common ground we're overlooking." Chances are that individual embodies the parrot style. Parrots tend to find the silver lining when situations take an unexpected turn. They boost morale and can turn a chaotic situation into an environment where people are engaged.

The DISC concept, though the terminology may be unfamiliar, aligns with our innate understanding of how we engage with others. We may describe ourselves as talkative or more inclined to listen attentively. In turn, we consider others' preferred modes of interaction, labeling them as gregarious or quiet. Accordingly, we adjust our communication style by speaking more deliberately or engaging in livelier conversations. However, inconsistencies arise when we fail to make these adaptations consistently.

The beauty of the DISC assessment lies in its ability to optimize our interactions beyond our comfort zones. It serves as a gentle reminder of our strengths and consistent tendencies. By heightening our awareness of our style and the perception we project onto others, we can make necessary adjustments to communicate effectively. In doing so, we assist others in understanding their own preferences and recognizing when their natural style proves ineffective.

It's a surreal experience of heightened situational awareness, acknowledging that we all encounter roles and responsibilities that lie beyond our comfort zone. Once we recognize these roles, we can consciously practice and develop our behavioral repertoire, ultimately paving the path to success.

As we continue to explore the depths of our behavioral styles, we master the art of genuine connection—a connection that surpasses mere words and leads to empathy and resonance. Armed with the knowledge of how others perceive the world, we can adapt our communication to meet them where they are to bridge the gaps that often divide us.

In this age of rapid globalization, diversity, and interconnectivity, the significance of effective communication cannot be overstated. It is the cornerstone upon which relationships flourish, teams thrive, and societies harmonize.

Through the power of the DISC assessment, we cultivate a heightened self-awareness and a deep understanding of our own strengths and areas for growth. We inculcate a genuine curiosity about others, recognizing that their perspectives, although different from our own, hold immeasurable value.

Final Thoughts

Having strong communication skills aids in all aspects of life— from one's professional to personal life and everything that falls in between. Effective communication is more difficult today than in the past because there are many more ways to connect. Because effective communication skills give you a deeper understanding of what others want and how to deliver information to them, they build strong work and personal relationships. With so many more choices of ways to communicate effectively, it is important to choose words carefully because things can become easily misinterpreted. Communicating effectively is a teachable skill; therefore, following a few of my tips, tidbits, and strategies outlined in this chapter will enable you to hone your communication skills.

So let us walk this path of effective communication with purpose and intention together. When everyone is on the same page about how they best communicate, there will be fewer misunderstandings and missed expectations, and people will feel heard and understood. Let us seek to comprehend before we seek to be understood, and listen before we speak.

Conclusion

We have reached the final chapter of Coaching From My Wheelchair: Tips, Tidbits, Tools, and Strategies for Improving Your Personal and Professional Self-development.

I am filled with a profound sense of gratitude and accomplishment after writing this book. Throughout this transformative voyage, we have explored the depths of personal growth, resilience, and the power of positive change.

From the very beginning, my purpose has been crystal clear— to empower you, the reader, on your personal and professional self- development. We set sail on this endeavor together, intertwining our stories, experiences, and insights. With each page turned, we uncovered the hidden treasures of positivity, resilience, and self- awareness that reside within us all.

Together, we discovered the immense power of positivity—the ability to forge a mindset that enhances the beauty of life and transcends our limitations. We explored the various obstacles that arise on our path, acknowledging their inevitability and harnessing the strength to overcome any obstacle with grace and determination.

Change, an ever-present force in our lives, becomes our ally as we make our way through the complexities of life's transitions. We unearth the importance of acceptance, seizing control of what we can, and pave a path forward through thoughtful action. With each step, we grow stronger and more resilient, ready to face the unknown with newly harnessed courage.

We acknowledge that learning is a lifelong pursuit, a never- ending journey of curiosity and personal expansion. We recognize the phenomenal power of adapting to new knowledge and the endless personal and professional opportunities that knowledge brings. The tales of Halloween traditions taught us valuable life lessons that enabled us to develop social skills, ignite creativity, and understand our audience in ways we never thought possible.

Venturing beyond our comfort zones, we discover a world brimming with growth and self-discovery. With HARPO as our guide, we embrace compelling reasons, acknowledge our fears, conduct research, choose challenging activities, and own our journey. Through the journey, the discomfort of the unknown becomes a catalyst for personal transformation, leading us to uncover our true potential.

In our pursuit of self-awareness, we peel back the layers of our being, shining a light on which traits require attention and growth. Through introspection and reflection, we recognize the importance of understanding ourselves fully. Armed with this knowledge, we evolve through self-discovery.

Knowing our strengths becomes the hallmark of our being as we discover the unique gifts that reside within us. We learn to harness our strengths, and we achieve true fulfillment and success.

By building new habits, we come to understand the immense power of consistency and routine. We craft habits that support our growth, replacing old patterns with positive ones. Through identification, time triggers, and subtasks, we witness how habits can reinforce the lessons learned throughout this book.

And now, as we reach the final pages of this book, I invite you to carry these lessons with you as you continue your journey. Remember St. Patrick's lesson of meeting people, which serves as a reminder to approach others with empathy, understanding, and compassion.

Appreciate the intricacies of human connection and strive to build bridges that bring us closer together rather than walls that keep us apart.

I came across some interesting facts about St. Patrick that beautifully exemplify the concept of meeting people where they are.

Little is known about his life, yet he lives on in popular culture as the saint who drove the snakes from Ireland and explained the Trinity using a shamrock. Whereas the snake story is a myth, the shamrock story holds a deeper meaning. Patrick used the shamrock to teach about the Trinity, presenting Christianity in a way that resonated with his audience. It may not have been a perfect representation, but it served to bridge the gap and ignite their curiosity and understanding. Meeting people where they are is a skill that highlights all aspects of our lives. It applies not only to our clients but also to every interaction we have with individuals from diverse backgrounds, cultures, and beliefs. Meeting people where they are makes up the art of connecting rather than projecting and engaging in dialogue that opens new pathways of understanding. Just as St. Patrick used storytelling to captivate and unite his audience, we, too, can embody the lessons of narratives to inspire, persuade, and create meaningful connections.

Furthermore, increasing our self-awareness is pivotal in meeting others where they are. Using our observational skills, we can better understand the circumstances and perspectives of those around us. Through keen observation, we gain insights that enable us to tailor our actions, stories, and explanations to resonate with their existing knowledge and experiences.

Remember, people are where they are, regardless of our desires for them to be different. By meeting people where they are, we honor their journey, promoting a sense of connection and understanding.

I extend to you my deepest appreciation for joining me on this extraordinary adventure of self-discovery and personal growth. May the lessons you have acquired guide you toward a future filled with purpose, fulfillment, and boundless possibilities.

With heartfelt gratitude and warm wishes,

Dr. Les Wright

References and Further Reading

Ackerman, C. E. (2020). *What is self-awareness? (+5 ways to be more self-aware)*. PositivePsychology.com. https://positivepsychology.com/self-awareness-matters- how-you-can-be-more-self-aware

American Psychological Association. (2019, December 12). *Students do better in school when they can understand, manage emotions.* https://www.apa.org/news/press/releases/2019/12/students- manage-emotions

Andreev, I. (2023, June 17). *Lifelong learning.* Valamis. https://www.valamis.com/hub/lifelong- learning#:~:text=Lifelong-learning-is-a-form,school- university-or-corporate-training

Arlinghaus, K. R., & Johnston, C. A. (2018). The importance of creating habits and routine. *American Journal of Lifestyle Medicine, 13*(2), 142–144. https://doi.org/10.1177/1559827618818044

Baker, L. (2020, October 9). *Why embracing change is the key to a good life.* BBC Culture. https://www.bbc.com/culture/article/20200930-why- embracing-change-is-the-key-to-a-good-life?zephr-modal- register

Balkhi, S. (2020, July 15). Five ways to learn more effectively. *Forbes.* https://www.forbes.com/sites/theyec/2020/07/15/five-ways- to-learn-more-effectively/?sh=20a4af393e7d

Baumeister, R. F., Bratslavsky, E., Finkenauer, C., & Vohs, K. D. (2001). Bad is stronger than good. *Review of General Psychology*, *5*(4), 323–370. https://doi.org/10.1037/1089-2680.5.4.323

Brenner, A. (2015, December 27). 5 benefits of stepping outside your comfort zone. *Psychology Today*. https://www.psychologytoday. com/us/blog/in-   flux/201512/5-benefits-stepping-outside-your-comfort-zone

Cherry, K. (2023, March 10). *What is self-awareness? Development, types, and how to improve.* Verywell Mind. https://www. verywellmind.com/what-is-self-awareness- 2795023

CLIMB Professional Development Training. (2019, July 19). *The 7 benefits of effective communication in personal and professional settings.* Portland Community College. https://climb.pcc.edu/ blog/the-7-benefits-of-effective-   communication-in-personal-and-professional-settings

Communication skills. (n.d.). Skills You Need. https://www. skillsyouneed.com/ips/communication- skills.html

Delony, J., & Ramsey, D. (2022). *Own your past, change your future: A not-so-complicated approach to relationships, mental health, and wellness.* Ramsey Press.

DePaul, K. (2021, February 2). What does it really take to build a new habit? *Harvard Business Review.* https://hbr.org/2021/02/what-does-it-really-take-to-build-a- new-habit

Dimachkie, M. M., & Barohn, R. J. (2014). Distal myopathies. *Neurologic Clinics*, *32*(3), 817–842. https://doi.org/10.1016/j.ncl.2014.04.004

Dweck, C. S. (2006). *Mindset: The new psychology of success.* Random House Digital.

Emmons, R. A., & McCullough, M. E. (2003). Counting blessings versus burdens: An experimental investigation of gratitude and subjective well-being in daily life. *Journal of Personality and Social Psychology, 84*(2), 377–389. https://doi.org/10.1037/0022-3514.84.2.377

Eurich, T. (2018, January 4). What self-awareness really is (and how to cultivate it). *Harvard Business Review.* https://hbr.org/2018/01/what-self-awareness-really-is-and- how-to-cultivate-it

Fincham, F. D., & Beach, S. R. (2010). Marriage in the new millennium: A decade in review. *Journal of Marriage and Family, 72*(3), 630–649.

Fortin VI, A. H., Dwamena, F., Frankel, R., Lepisto, B., & Smith, R. (2019). *Smith's patient-centered interviewing: An evidence-based method* (4th ed.). McGraw-Hill.

Fredrickson, B. L. (2001). The role of positive emotions in positive psychology: The broaden-and-build theory of positive emotions. *American Psychologist, 56*(3), 218–226. https://doi.org/10.1037/0003-066X.56.3.218

Fredrickson, B. L. (2004). The broaden-and-build theory of positive emotions. *Philosophical Transactions of the Royal Society of London. Series B: Biological Sciences, 359*(1449), 1367–1377. https://doi.org/10.1098/rstb.2004.1512

Fredrickson, B. L., Tugade, M. M., Waugh, C. E., & Larkin, G. R. (2003). What good are positive emotions in crises? A prospective study of resilience and emotions following the terrorist attacks on the United States on September 11th, 2001. *Journal of Personality and Social Psychology, 84*(2), 365–376. https://doi.org/10.1037//0022-3514.84.2.365

Frodsham, J. (2020, June 30). Council post: Helping clients realize sustainable change through targeted coaching. *Forbes.* https://www.forbes.com/sites/forbescoachescouncil/2020/0   6/30/helping-clients-realize-sustainable-change-through-   targeted-coaching/?sh=555d2a173986

Gable, S. L., Reis, H. T., Impett, E. A., & Asher, E. R. (2004). What do you do when things go right? The intrapersonal and interpersonal benefits of sharing positive events.

Journal of Personality and Social Psychology, 87(2), 228–245. https://doi.org/10.1037/0022-3514.87.2.228 Gianaros, P. J., Horenstein, J. A., Cohen, S., Matthews, K. A.,

Brown, S. M., Flory, J. D., Critchley, H. D., Manuck, S. B., & Hariri, A. R. (2007). Perigenual anterior cingulate morphology covaries with perceived social standing. *Social Cognitive and Affective Neuroscience, 2*(3), 161–173. https://doi.org/10.1093/scan/nsm013

Glaser, R., & Kiecolt-Glaser, J. K. (2005). Stress-induced immune dysfunction: Implications for health. *Nature Reviews Immunology, 5*(3), 243–251. https://doi.org/10.1038/nri1571

Gringras, P., Middleton, B., Skene, D. J., & Revell, V. L. (2015).

Bigger, brighter, bluer—better? Current light-emitting devices—Adverse sleep properties and preventative strategies. *Frontiers in Public Health, 3,* 233.

HandaGupta, S. (2020, November 4). *Coaching for change.* International Coaching Federation. https://coachingfederation.org/blog/coaching-for-change

Hartemann, A., Bensimon, G., Payan, C., Jacqueminet, S., Bourron, O., Nicolas, N., Fonfrede, M., Rosenzwajg, M., Bernard, C., &

Klatzmann, D. (2013). Low-dose interleukin 2 in patients with type 1 diabetes: A phase 1/2 randomised, double-blind, placebo-controlled trial. *The Lancet Diabetes & Endocrinology, 1*(4), 295–305. https://doi.org/10.1016/s2213-8587(13)70113-x

Hedlund, U. (2013, September 16). *Communicate effectively leveraging DISC profiles.* Business Productivity. https://businessproductivity. com/communicate-effectively- leveraging-disc-profiles

Henson, B. et al. (2023). *Why DISC by Take Flight Learning?*

Discover eagles, parrots, doves & owls: Styles that stick. Take Flight Learning. https://takeflightlearning.com Huang, Y., Humphreys, B. R., & Lee, J. (2016). A dynamic analysis of the role of happiness in the relation between exercise and mental health in younger and older adults. *Health Economics, 25*(12), 1521.

Jackson, J. (2017, March 20). Why willingness to learn is the key to success. *Forbes.* https://www.forbes.com/sites/ jpmorganchase/2017/03/20/w hy-willingness-to-learn-is-the-key-to- success/?sh=13cad56818a0

Jha, P. (2020). The hazards of smoking and the benefits of cessation: A critical summation of the epidemiological evidence in high-income countries. *eLife, 9,* e49979.

Krokoff, L. J., Epperson, D. L., & Hastie, R. (2010). The predictive effects of negative marital interactions on divorce: A multilevel modeling approach. *Journal of Marriage and Family, 72*(3), 666–679. https://doi.org/10.1111/j.1741-3737.2010.00723.x

Lancaster, A. (2022) *Why is communication important?* Mallory. https:// mallory.com.au/cm/why-is-communication- important

Latham, A. (2018, April 11). 16 reasons why you should get out of your comfort zone now. *Forbes.* https://www.forbes.com/sites/

annlatham/2018/04/11/16- reasons-why-you-should-get-out-of-your-comfort-zone- now/?sh=4ea26bed62e5

Lau, Y. (2021, September 30). Embrace lifelong learning to thrive in the future of work. *Forbes.* https://www.forbes.com/sites/forbeshumanresourcescouncil /2021/09/30/embrace-lifelong-learning-to-thrive-in-the- future-of-work/?sh=24b6d86d7631

Lerner, J. S., & Keltner, D. (2001). Fear, anger, and risk. *Journal of Personality and Social Psychology*, *81*(1), 146–159. https://doi.org/10.1037/0022-3514.81.1.146

Louie, D., Brook, K., & Frates, E. (2016). The laughter prescription: A tool for lifestyle medicine. *American Journal of Lifestyle Medicine*, *10*(4), 262–267. https://doi.org/10.1177/1559827614550279

Lyubomirsky, S., King, L., & Diener, E. (2005). The benefits of frequent positive affect: Does happiness lead to success? *Psychological Bulletin*, *131*(6), 803–855. https://doi.org/10.1037/0033-2909.131.6.803

Magnus-Sharpe, S. (2022, March 29). Leaving your comfort zone inspires motivation, growth. *Cornell Chronicle.* https://news.cornell.edu/stories/2022/03/leaving-your- comfort-zone-inspires-motivation-growth

Mandolesi, L., Polverino, A., Montuori, S., Foti, F., Ferraioli, G., Sorrentino, P., & Sorrentino, G. (2018). Effects of physical exercise on cognitive functioning and wellbeing: Biological and psychological benefits. *Frontiers in Psychology*, *9*. http://doi.org/10.3389/fpsyg.2018.00509

Manson, M. (n.d.). *Habits: The definitive guide to building good habits and breaking bad ones*. Mark Manson. https://markmanson.net/habits

Marino, A. (2020, February 18). How to build healthy habits that last. *The New York Times*. https://www.nytimes.com/2020/02/18/ well/mind/how-to- build-healthy-habits.html

Marom, L. (2022, April 6). How to build a culture of learning.*Forbes*. https://www.forbes.com/sites/forbescoachescouncil/2022/0 4/06/ how-to-build-a-culture-of-learning/?sh=1304f32a1efa

McGarvey, S. (2022). *Ignite a shift: Engaging minds, guiding emotions and driving behavior*. Morgan James Publishing.

Milkman, K. (2021, November 29). *How to build habits that stick in 5 steps*. CNN. https://edition.cnn.com/2021/11/29/health/5-steps-habit- builder-wellness/index.html

MindTools Content Team. (n.d). *Coaching through change*. MindTools. https://www.mindtools.com/agjj594/coaching- through-change

Molinsky, A. (2016, July 29). If you're not outside your comfort zone, you won't learn anything. *Harvard Business Review.* https://hbr. org/2016/07/if-youre-not-outside-your-comfort- zone-you-wont-learn-anything

Ohlin, B. (2023, March 27). *7 ways to improve communication in relationships*. PositivePsychology.com. https:// positivepsychology.com/communication-in- relationships

Parker, S. (2021, July 15). The science of habits. *Knowable Magazine*. https://knowablemagazine.org/article/mind/2021/the- science-habits

Pascal, A., Sass, M., & Gregory, J. B. (2015). I'm only human: The role of technology in coaching. *Consulting Psychology Journal: Practice and Research*, *67*(2), 100–109. https://doi.org/10.1037/ cpb0000025

Practice.(2022,September 12).*Top 5 benefits of developing communication skills*. https://practice.do/blog/benefits-of- communication-skills

Rosenberg, Merrick. (2015). *Taking flight!: Master the DISC styles to transform your career, your relationships . . . your life. Financial Times* Pren Hall. https://merrickrosenberg.com/

Rothman, N. B., Caza, B. B., Melwani, S., & Walsh, K. (2021, September 14). Embracing the power of ambivalence. *Harvard Business Review.* https://hbr.org/2021/09/embracing-the-power-of-ambivalence

Ruch, W., Martínez-Martí, M. L., Proyer, R. T., & Harzer, C. (2014). The character strengths rating form (CSRF): Development and initial assessment of a 24-item rating scale to assess character strengths. *Personality and Individual Differences, 68*, 53–58.

Segerstrom, S. C., & Miller, G. E. (2004). Psychological stress and the human immune system: A meta-analytic study of 30 years of inquiry. *Psychological Bulletin, 130*(4), 601–630. https://doi.org/10.1037/0033-2909.130.4.601

Seligman, M. E. (2011). *Flourish: A visionary new understanding of happiness and well-being.* Free Press.

Simone, P. M., & Scuilli, M. (2006). Cognitive benefits of participation in lifelong learning institutes. *The LLI Review, 1*(1), 44–51.

Smith, R. (2021, October 2). *How to effectively communicate with others.* Psychology Today. https://www.psychologytoday.com/intl/blog/patient- zero/202110/how-effectively-communicate-others

Spector, P. E., & Fox, S. (2005). The stressor-emotion model of counterproductive work behavior. In S. Fox & P. E. Spector (Eds.), *Counterproductive work behavior: Investigations of actors and targets* (pp. 151–174).

American Psychological Association. https://doi.org/10.1037/10893-008

Sy, J., & Cruz, N. (2019). Life outside your comfort zone. *Journal of International Students, 9*(4), 1203–1208. https://doi.org/10.32674/jis.v9i4.1022

Talerico, A. (2023, February 16). *The importance of lifelong learning.* Corporate Finance Institute. https://corporatefinanceinstitute. com/resources/elearning/th e-importance-of-lifelong-learning/

Tindle, H. A., Chang, Y. F., Kuller, L. H., Manson, J. E.,

Robinson, J. G., Rosal, M. C., & Matthews, K. A. (2009). Optimism, cynical hostility, and incident coronary heart disease and mortality in the Women's Health Initiative. *Circulation, 120*(8), 656–662. https://doi.org/10.1161/CIRCULATIONAHA.108.827642

Todd, B. (2021, March). *How to identify your personal strengths.* 80,000 Hours. https://80000hours.org/articles/personal-strengths

Vozza, S. (2022, July 19). How to become more open-minded and willing to change. *Fast Company.* https://www.fastcompany. com/90769632/how-to-become- more-open-minded-and-willing-to-change

Whitmore, J. (2017). *Coaching for performance: Growing human potential and purpose: The principles and practice of coaching and leadership.* Nicholas Brealey.

Wood, J. V., Perunovic, W. Q., & Lee, J. W. (2009). Positive self-statements: Power for some, peril for others. *Psychological Science, 20*(7), 860–866. https://doi.org/10.1111/j.1467-9280.2009.02370.x

Zhang, Y., & Chen, M. (2018). Character strengths, strengths use, future self-continuity and subjective well-being among Chinese University students. *Frontiers in Psychology, 9*, 10-40. https://doi.org/10.3389/fpsyg.2018.01040

www.ingramcontent.com/pod-product-compliance
Lightning Source LLC
Chambersburg PA
CBHW071012120626
46546CB00003B/1050

* 9 7 8 1 9 6 2 6 2 4 0 7 7 *